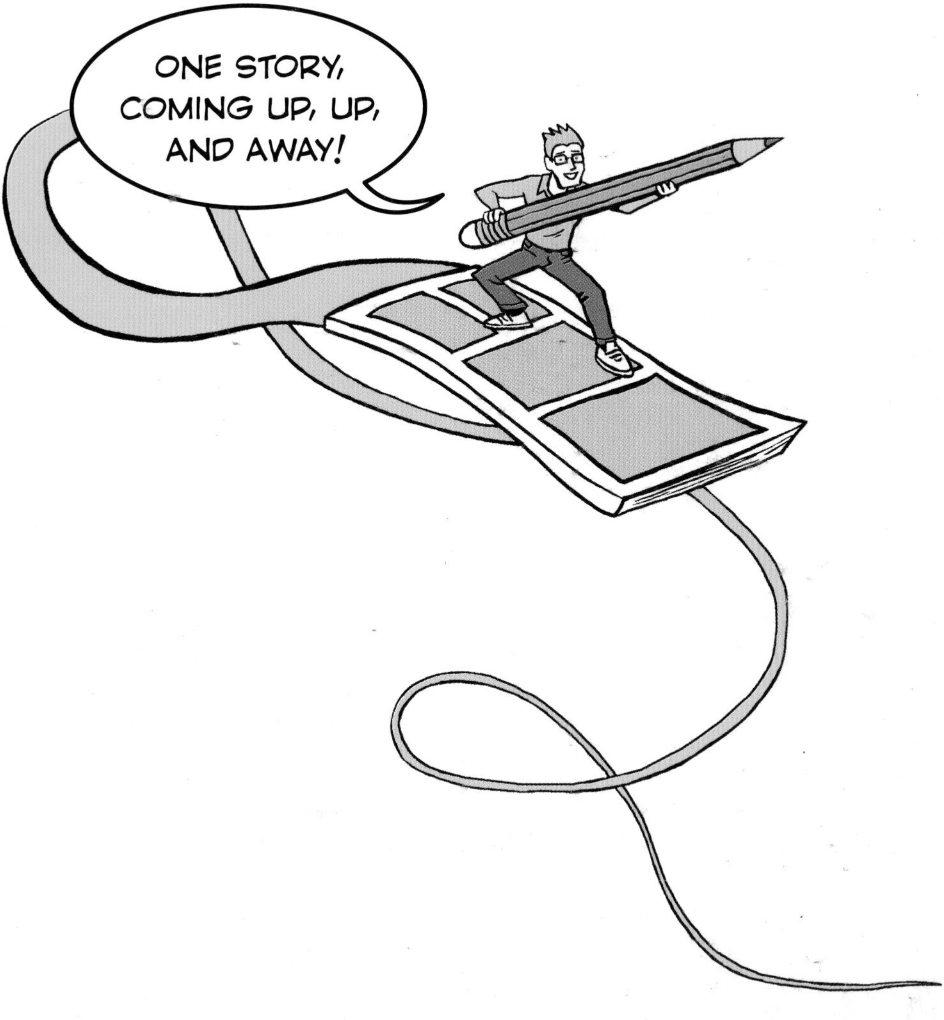
ONE STORY, COMING UP, UP, AND AWAY!

To my mom, who was the best teacher to all her students, especially me.

And to Will Eisner and Scott McCloud, who really started the conversation about what makes comics tick.

Owlkids Books acknowledges the financial support of the Canada Council for the Arts, the Ontario Arts Council, the Government of Canada through the Canada Book Fund (CBF) and the Government of Ontario through the Ontario Media Development Corporation's Book Initiative for our publishing activities.

Published in Canada by
Owlkids Books Inc.
10 Lower Spadina Avenue
Toronto, ON M5V 2Z2

Published in the United States by
Owlkids Books Inc.
1700 Fourth Street
Berkeley, CA 94710

Library and Archives Canada Cataloguing in Publication
McLachlan, Brian
    Draw out the story : ten secrets to creating your own comics / Brian McLachlan.

Includes index.
ISBN 978-1-926973-83-8 (bound).--ISBN 978-1-77147-003-2 (pbk.)

    1. Comic books, strips, etc.--Authorship--Juvenile literature. 2. Comic books, strips, etc.--Technique--Juvenile literature. 3. Comic books, strips, etc.--Illustrations--Juvenile literature. 4. Drawing--Technique--Juvenile literature. I. Title.

PN6710.M46 2013   j741.5'1   C2012-908501-4

Library of Congress Control Number: 2013930987

Design: Barb Kelly, Michel Vrana

Manufactured in Shenzhen, China, in March 2013, by Printplus Limited
Job #5747A

A   B   C   D   E   F

Publisher of Chirp, chickaDEE and OWL
www.owlkidsbooks.com

DRAW OUT THE STORY

TEN SECRETS
TO CREATING YOUR OWN
COMICS

BY BRIAN McLACHLAN

CONTENTS!

SECRET **Five** Let the PERSONALITY shine

PAGE **59**

SECRET **Six** Take it ONE MOMENT at a time

PAGE **71**

SECRET **Seven** Know your TOOLS

PAGE **83**

SECRET **Eight** You need more than one GOOD IDEA

PAGE **99**

SECRET **Nine** There are 2 ways to build a story

PAGE **113**

SECRET **Ten** Go BEYOND the normal

PAGE **129**

CONCLUSION

PAGE **140**

WELCOME!

There are ten secrets to making great comics. But underneath those ten is maybe the most important secret of all:

Comics are all about telling stories.

Just like music, films, and novels, comics are a way to share a message. How you draw, use word balloons, and design characters are all important, but they're not the main thing. What matters is whether each element helps tell your story.

Comics can tell any kind of story. Whether you want to create a horror or comedy, biography or fantasy, all comics use the same building blocks to move the story from your mind to the page.

There are a million things to learn about making comics, but at their heart, comics are actually very simple. Just as you can do so much with only 26 letters in the alphabet, or six strings on a guitar, you can use these ten secrets to build an endless amount of different stories.

So here are the ten secrets and some fun ways to try them out for yourself. If you are ever unsure what to do in your comic, come back to the question "Does this make the story better?" The reason you're making a comic is to share a story, right?

Now let's get cracking!

MY STORY BEGINS...

WHEN I WAS EIGHT YEARS OLD, MY COMIC DRAWING WAS PUBLISHED THANKS TO AN ART CONTEST IN OWL MAGAZINE.

THIRTY YEARS LATER, I'M WRITING ABOUT COMICS FOR OWLKIDS BOOKS. YOU NEVER KNOW HOW FAR COMICS CAN TAKE YOU.

ALONG THE WAY, I'VE DRAWN FOR NEWSPAPERS, GRAPHIC NOVELS, WEBCOMICS, AND TEXTBOOKS.

YOU MAY HAVE EVEN DRAWN MUSTACHES ON MY ARTWORK!

COMICS HAVE TAKEN ME MANY PLACES.

I'VE TESTED OUT THESE TEN SECRETS SO THAT WHEREVER YOU GO, THEY SHOULD WORK FOR YOU, TOO.

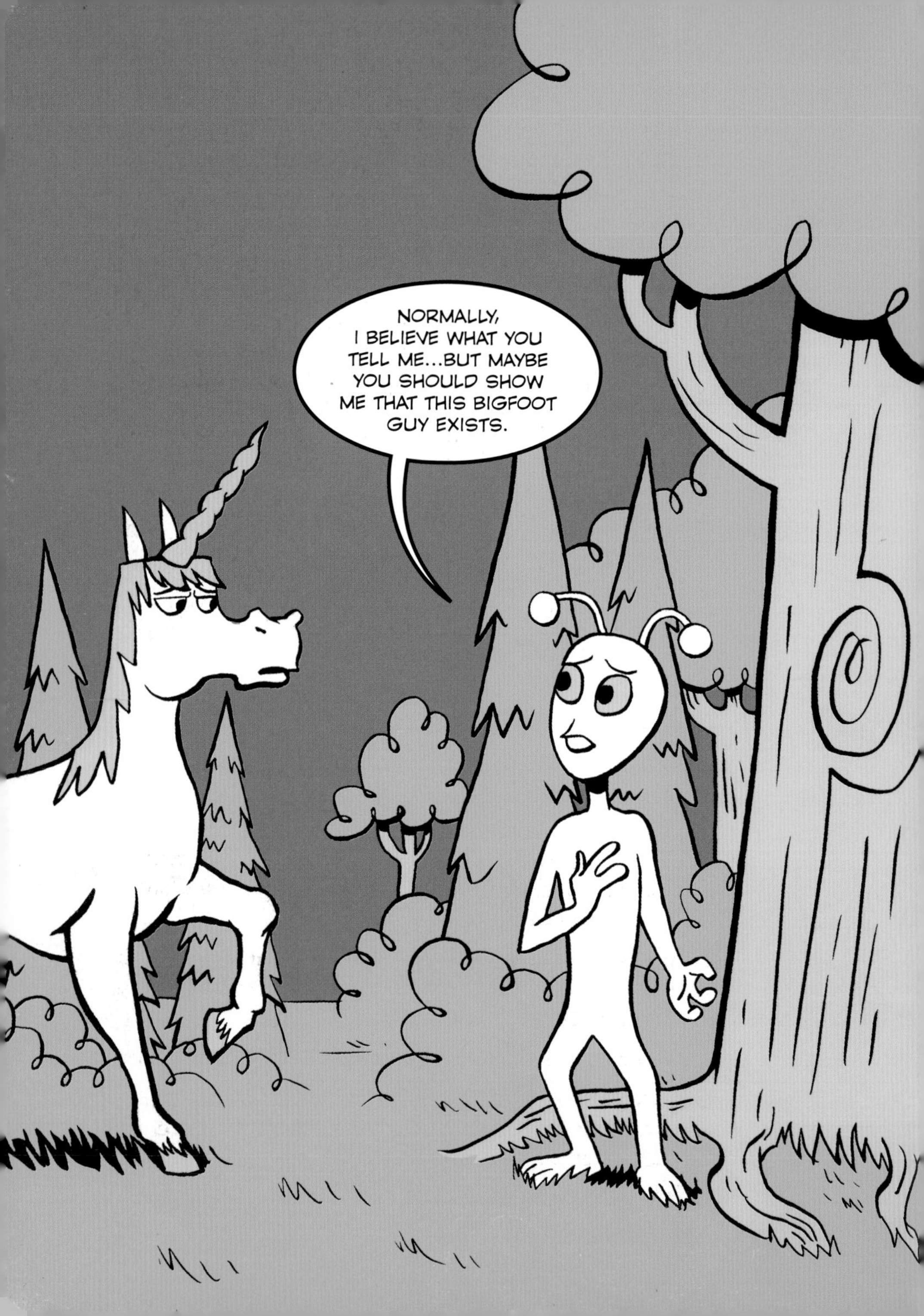
NORMALLY, I BELIEVE WHAT YOU TELL ME...BUT MAYBE YOU SHOULD SHOW ME THAT THIS BIGFOOT GUY EXISTS.

COMICS let you SHOW & TELL

SECRET ONE

Comics use pictures and words together in a way that makes them different from anything else.

Have you ever been telling people about some amazing place you went, except you can't really put your experience into words? If only you had a photograph to help explain what you saw, right?

Or have you shown people a photograph of a hilarious moment from your vacation, but still had to explain why it was so funny? "That waiter was so weird! He kept offering us the 'soap of the day.'"

You see, sometimes pictures and words just can't do the job on their own.

Comics marry **pictures and words** to let you tell more of the story than either can on its own. They let you both **show** (with pictures) *and* **tell** (with words). What does that mean? Let's use the example of Robin Hood to examine how pictures and words work.

What can pictures do?

Pictures are really good at showing you a **moment in time**. Imagine a fine art painting of Robin and his Merry Men like this (or even larger!).

They say a **picture is worth a thousand words,** and you could spend a million describing the exact details captured in this one image. But what happened before and after the moment shown in the picture? To know that, you'd need more pictures... or words.

10

What can words do?

The novels you find on most library shelves are really good at showing a **span of time** (in other words, a lot longer than just one moment). For example, most Robin Hood adventures follow the same basic pattern:

Robin Hood assembles a group of fellow outlaws. He is outbattled by Little John and outwitted by Friar Tuck, and then gains the admiration of the youthful Will Scarlet. They work together to steal from the rich and give to the poor. This upsets the greedy Sheriff of Nottingham, who offers a reward for Robin's capture. In disguise, Robin enters an archery contest during May Day to win the heart of the May Queen, Maid Marian. Robin rescues Marian from the Sheriff and escapes into Sherwood Forest with the help of his loyal Merry Men.

You could make a hundred paintings and still not capture all the emotions, actions, and reactions that words describe in this story. But what exactly does Sherwood Forest look like? For that, you'd need more words... or pictures.

Pictures + words + ??

So comics combine pictures and words. A picture in a Robin Hood comic could show you that Robin wore a green hat with a feather in it. The words will tell you other details, like "He kept a secret skeleton key in his boot." But there is a third way of communicating with readers that makes comics unique—a group of elements that includes word balloons, panels, sound effects, and more. I like to call these elements **comics grammar**.

These elements act a lot like periods, commas, and semicolons do in writing—they help guide the reader. That's why a children's Robin Hood picture book can use pictures and words and yet still not be a comic. It's not using comics grammar.

But if Robin speaks in word balloons, and horses go ***CLIP! CLOP!*** as they trot, it becomes a comic. Just like normal grammar, **comics grammar** gives words and pictures the **flavor and rules** that make them a comic.

A COMICS GRAMMAR LESSON

Here are some of the important parts of comics grammar—these ones are like the periods, commas, and question marks of comics.

CAPTION BOX: where the narrator's voice goes

SPEECH BALLOON: what a character is saying

MIDNIGHT, IN TOLTEM FOREST

THOUGHT BALLOON: what a character is thinking

ME EAT YOUR FACE!

TAIL: It leads to the speaker or thinker of the balloon

I'M DOOMED!

SOUND EFFECTS: words that show noises

SPLOSH!

PANEL: the box a comic is told in

PANEL BORDER: the outline of the box

Comics give some details and story...and let the reader imagine the rest

With a comic, the reader has to **imagine some of the visual details**, because the drawings are simpler and smaller than most paintings and photographs. The reader also has to **imagine some of the story**, because there are fewer words used to tell it. And the comic panels invite the reader to imagine what has happened between them.

Here we see three different moments of time from a Robin Hood adventure comic.

ROBIN! LITTLE JOHN'S BEEN IMPRISONED IN THE CASTLE!
LET'S BREAK HIM OUT!
HOW DID WE GET HERE WITH THESE COSTUMES?
THAT'S FOR THE READER TO IMAGINE.

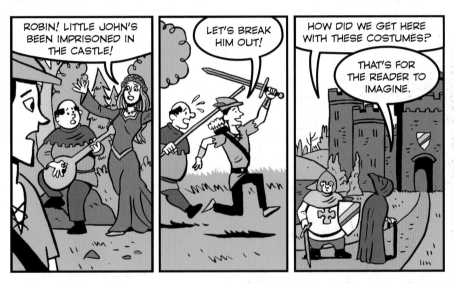

Despite the **small amount** of visuals and text, the reader is actually given a lot of information here. The trick of cartooning is giving readers enough details for the story, but not too many or too few. Of course, artists have different ideas of what's too simple and what's too detailed. **How much detail** you put in is not only up to you, it helps to define your style, too.

Don't repeat yourself

So if comics are words and pictures together, you must decide when—and how—to use one or the other. A good rule of thumb is to let one add to the other, not repeat what has already been shown or said.

Which is best to use?

If pictures can give the reader specific visual details, words can give specific information and thoughts. Knowing this will help you figure out when it's clearer to draw something and when it's clearer to write it.

Active reading

When you read comics, be an **active reader**. Don't just think about what's happening and wonder how the story will end. Think about how the cartoonist made the story. How much does the artist draw? How much does he rely on words? What types of lines does she make? What do you think works? What would make it better?

It's easier to practice active reading with comics you've already read once. Then you can see how the cartoonist built the comic to its ending.

If you don't read a lot of comics, start by exploring your favorite books, web comics, newspaper strips, and graphic novels.

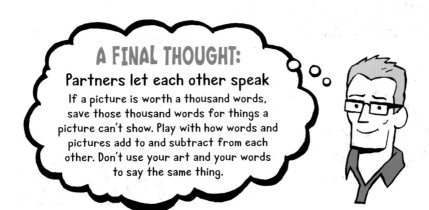

A FINAL THOUGHT:

Partners let each other speak

If a picture is worth a thousand words, save those thousand words for things a picture can't show. Play with how words and pictures add to and subtract from each other. Don't use your art and your words to say the same thing.

FIRST COMICS

Let's not waste any time!

Let's make some comics right away by combining pictures and words.

1a. Cut a page into four equal quarters.

b. On each quarter draw two characters: a cop and a robber, two animals, two objects from a desk (add eyes and mouths), and you and a friend (or pick your own duo).

×8

c. Cut out eight oval word balloons with tails.

d. Pick a bunch of sentences at random. You could flip through a book and plop your finger on a phrase. You might skip forward through a song or movie to see what lyrics or lines of dialogue appear. Or you could use phrases you've overheard, or ask people for suggestions.

e. Put those sentences into the eight different word balloons.

f. Put each balloon over a character's head. See what combinations you can make. What effect does it have to combine pictures with words? Are any of these combinations funny? Weird? Scary? Boring? Confusing?

g. Do any of the combinations give you ideas about what else you could draw in the box to have the sentence make more sense? Go ahead and add them.

h. Do you have ideas for other sentences that would be more interesting? Flip the balloon over and use them instead.

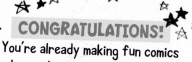

CONGRATULATIONS!
You're already making fun comics by combining words, pictures, and comics grammar!

2 Now photocopy or scan a few comics. White out the word balloons and make up your own words to create a new story.

PICK YOUR OWN
1 + 2 + 3

STYLE	GENRE	FORMAT
MANGA	SUPERHERO	GRAPHIC NOVEL
PHOTOREALISM	SPORTS	COMIC BOOK
POINTILISM	MARTIAL ARTS	STRIP
IMPRESSIONISM	SPY	ANTHOLOGY
SURREALISM	ROMANCE	WEBCOMIC
RETRO	HORROR	ONE-PANEL

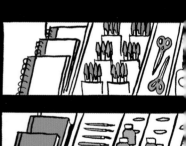

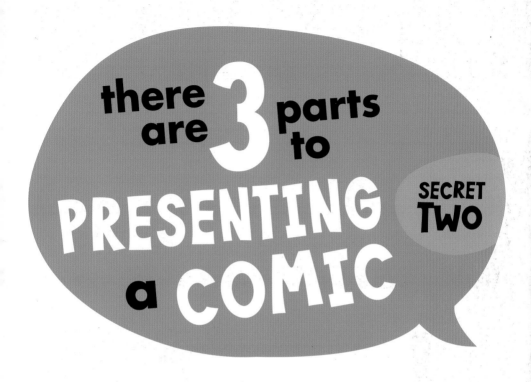

there are **3** parts to

PRESENTING a COMIC

SECRET TWO

When you make a comic, there are three key elements to think about. What are they?

Style is how your comic appears visually. Do you draw very realistically with a brush? Do you draw very loosely with chalk?

Genre is the category your comic belongs to. Are you making a comedy? A crime story? A superhero comic?

Format is how the comic is presented physically, and how long it is. Is it a comic strip? A comic book? A graphic novel?

For example, you could tell Hercules's story in the style of pixel-art, in the genre of western, and the format of a comic strip. This is how it might look.

Now, what if you told Hercules's story with a different style, genre, and format? Perhaps a painted, sci-fi graphic novel? It would be a very different version, right?

Different styles, different messages

In the real world, your choice of words changes depending on who you talk to. You might be polite when speaking to your principal but use slang with your best buddy. The same idea goes for when you're writing your comic—you need to think carefully about the words you choose. What words will best suit certain situations or characters?

A style of art may also fit better in certain places than others. In fact, the way you draw might even change the genre of story you're telling. Think of all the silly cartoon characters who've been crushed by falling safes, anvils, and rocks. When that big-eyed, goofy-looking guy gets hit with a piano, it's funny partly because he doesn't seem real.

But what if that same scene was drawn to look more like a real person and a real piano? That wouldn't be a comedy anymore—it would be a horror story. The accident would seem too real.

Utensils tell a story, too

Your style also changes depending on your **utensils**, or what you use to draw with. A cartoon drawn with crayon on lined paper won't seem as serious as one drawn with a technical pen on blank paper. A story told in full color will be more vibrant than one told in black and white.

Experiment with different drawing utensils to learn what each does well—and what suits you best.

Most of the comics in this book were inked with a **brush pen** that uses disposable ink cartridges. This pen makes lines that go from thick to thin, without the mess of dipping a regular brush in ink.

Six slick styles

There are lots of styles you can use to draw your story, like **manga**, **romance**, **funny animal**, and more. You can also get inspired by other types of art, like sculpture, fashion, or even tattoos. Here are six examples of styles to get you thinking.

High Contrast

If you use brushes, markers, or a computer, you can **fill in** wide-open areas with **black**. It's great for making stories dramatic, scary, and moody.

High Impact

Use **action lines** and dynamic angles to make an intense comic where characters seem to leap out at the reader. This is great for action-adventure, superhero, and martial arts comics.

Environmental

Draw the setting with at least as much **detail** as the characters in it. This is great for fantasy, sci-fi, and stories set in unusual environments, because it shows all the unfamiliar details.

Fumetti

Can't draw? Got a **camera**? Try fumetti. You can even build fun things to photograph or touch up images with computer effects. This is great for stories set in the real world.

Stick Figure

Many great cartoonists use only the **bare bones** to tell their stories. Stick figures are good for nearly any story, because your reader imagines the awesome parts.

I made all these comics to show that you can draw in many styles, not just one!

Crafty

Do you like to make **crafts**? You can use construction paper, scissors, glue, and sparkles to create images. It's good for charming or simple stories.

Genres

Genres help **categorize stories**. Your comic can fit in any genre, from romance to horror.

You don't have to pick a genre. After all, life isn't one genre. We all have moments of comedy, adventure, drama, and mystery. You can just tell a story and let other people decide what genre it is. But thinking about genres can inspire new ideas. Here are some examples of genres, organized according to their focus.

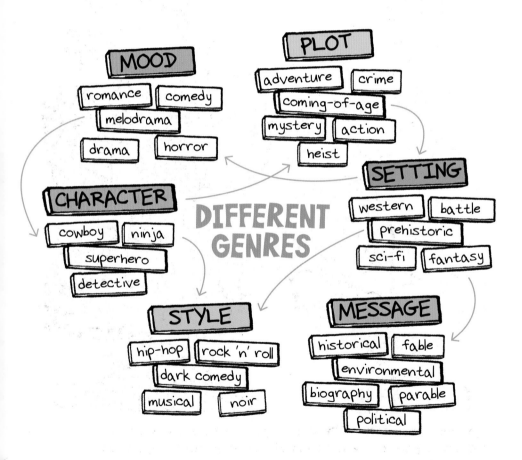

Here's the fun part: you can **mix and match** genres in any way you like to find a combination that is exciting to you.

People already combine genres for romantic comedies and war dramas. Why not mix hip-hop and sci-fi for a rap/dance battle across the galaxies? Or mash up romance and crime to create a cops-and-robbers tale where someone's heart is stolen. Or throw together western, heist, parable, horror, and musical to tell a rhyming story about why you shouldn't steal from cactus monsters!

In other words, when you're searching for your voice, you can try techniques proven to work or experiment with something new and exciting. It's up to you.

Seven slick formats

Many **shapes** and **sizes** of comics have become popular for telling stories. These are called formats. Again, you can decide which format tells your story best. Each format has its own strengths. Let's go back to Robin Hood to guide us.

Single Panel

It's a one-panel comic, sometimes with no panel border, and not many words.

Examples: *The Family Circus, The Far Side, New Yorker* magazine comics

Great for: Quick observations, especially jokes, and cartoonists who have lots of ideas but don't focus as much on character and plot.

Robin as single-panel comic: You might notice that the name of Robin's home forest is a pun for saying "Yes!"

I STEAL FROM THE RICH AND GIVE TO THE POOR!
I'M RICH!
CLINK!
AWRIGHT, STICK 'EM UP!

Comic Strip

It's a comic that's more than one panel, in one or more rows, but not more than one page long.

Examples: *Bizarro, Peanuts, For Better or For Worse*

Great for: Anecdotes, like stories you'd tell your friends about what happened during your day.

Robin as comic strip: The strip shows a moment when Robin gets confused while stealing from the rich and giving to the poor.

Anthology

It's a book of several different comic stories. The stories are usually tied together by a theme or a shared world.

Examples: *Archie Digest, Max Finder Mystery, Weekly Shonen Jump*

Great for: Telling many different stories, sometimes even with different characters.

Robin as anthology: You might have an eight-page forest robbery, a four-page story of Friar Tuck making dinner, and two pages of Robin trying on disguises.

PRO TIP

Most cartoonists color with a computer. It makes it easy to get very flat, even coloring, or gradients, that would take a long time to achieve with paint, colored pencils, pastel, or other coloring tools.

THE FEAST
THE END

Comic Book

Usually a **20- or 24-page** comic book is called an **issue**. Sometimes each book is a story on its own, but sometimes it's part of a series of books. Comic book stories are sometimes collected into **graphic novels**.

Examples: *Uncanny X-Men, Bone, Wonder Woman*

Great for: Telling short stories or chapters of a longer story.

Robin as comic book: One issue might show that a new, worthy adversary has joined the Merry Men. Or it might show the first part of a longer story about Robin being captured, with the next issue showing him being rescued.

Graphic Novel

Usually **at least 80 pages** long, graphic novels are stories with a lot of plot and character development and a planned conclusion.

Examples: *The Adventures of Tintin, Ghostopolis, Two Generals*

Great for: Stories with great depth and creators with lots of patience (even pros can spend years on one graphic novel).

Robin as graphic novel: He might defeat the Sheriff so thoroughly that Prince John hires a new, meaner Sheriff...whom the old Sheriff helps to defeat. Or it might be about how Robin grew from boy to man.

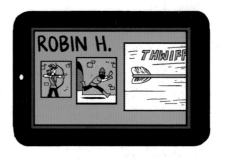

Web Comics

Web comics can be **any of these formats**, but they are put on the web instead of on paper. Unlike in a book, **each page of a web comic can be a different size**, from one tiny panel to a long, scrolling maze.

Examples: *The Abominable Charles Christopher, Lunchbox Funnies,* and my own, *The Princess Planet*

Of course, you can **use any format** or **create your own**, from choose-your-own-adventure stories to comic panels that make a board game—or **anything else your mind can imagine**!

Hybrids

Part comic, **part novel**, hybrids use elements of both. This approach allows the parts that work best as text and as comic do their thing.

Examples: *Frankie Pickle, Thieves & Kings, Captain Underpants*

Great for: Cartoonists who like to write as much as they like to draw.

Robin as hybrid: A Robin hybrid might use text to explain his thought process, while comic panels can be used to show a chase scene across the top of a castle.

A FINAL THOUGHT:
Stay true to your story

The style, genre, and format you choose help present your story to readers. Each choice you make can support or work against the others. If you keep that in mind, you'll be better prepared to pick the right combination for the story you're telling.

YOUR TURN

TRACING AND STYLES

Now that you know the three parts
to presenting a comic, let's explore styles, genres,
and formats with some fun activities.

1 Look for comics in libraries, newspapers, and magazines;
on the internet; at bookstores and comic conventions; and
anywhere else you can find them.

Pick five artists you like.

Make a list of what you like about the way they draw.

2 Choose one of the artists you like.

Trace the artist's work. You'll probably want to photocopy
it—or use a printout if it's from the web—then tape a
piece of tracing paper over it. This way you can rotate the
page when it helps.

PRO TIP

Some people complain
that tracing is copying,
but that's how you learn.
When you're starting out,
copying how other people
do it is a really valuable
exercise. Just don't brag
that your traced drawings
are your own originals!

As you draw, be an active observer—of
both the original and your own drawing.

- How does your hand move as you
  trace the image?

- Is there a better way to move
  your hand?

- How does the artist balance
  black and white?

- What lines does he or she use
  to show texture?

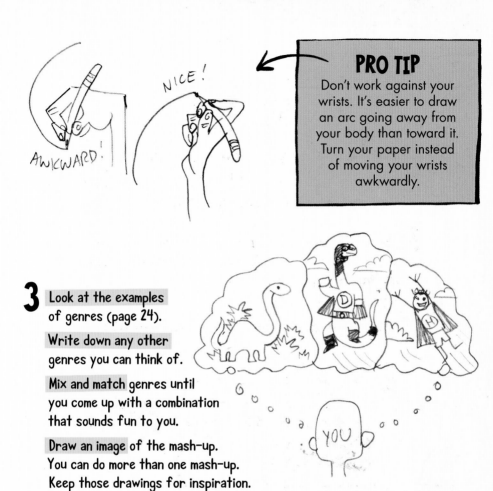

AWKWARD!

NICE!

PRO TIP

Don't work against your wrists. It's easier to draw an arc going away from your body than toward it. Turn your paper instead of moving your wrists awkwardly.

3 Look at the examples of genres (page 24).

Write down any other genres you can think of.

Mix and match genres until you come up with a combination that sounds fun to you.

Draw an image of the mash-up. You can do more than one mash-up. Keep those drawings for inspiration.

YOU

4 Think about what comics you already enjoy.

Make a list. Write down what format they fit into.

Write down what genre or genres you think they are.

What format would you have the most fun doing?

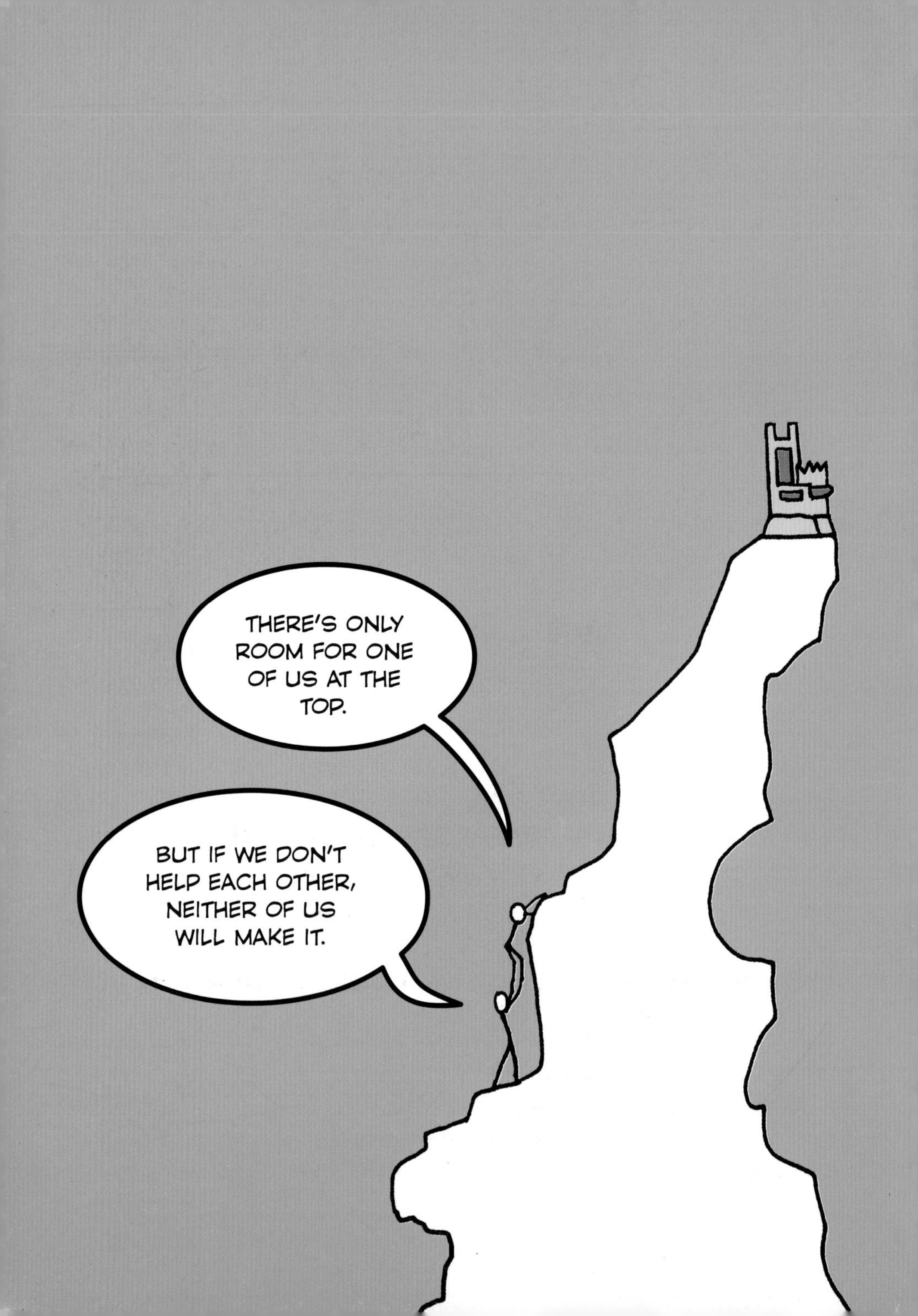
THERE'S ONLY ROOM FOR ONE OF US AT THE TOP.
BUT IF WE DON'T HELP EACH OTHER, NEITHER OF US WILL MAKE IT.

SIMPLE ART doesn't equal SIMPLE STORIES

It's not about how well you can draw. It's about how well people can understand what you draw.

When people hear the word "artist," they often think of someone who paints portraits or landscapes. (OK, an artist can do a lot more than that, but bear with me...) This type of artist's main goal is to capture what the eyes see, much like a camera.

We know a cartoonist's main goal is to tell a story. How does telling a story with comics make a **cartoonist** different from a **fine artist**? Let's have a look.

A Fine Artist:

- *puts a lot of work into one large image*

- *has only one chance to show you what's in a scene*

- *makes art that is studied by careful observation*

- *has to draw or paint the final details only once*

A Cartoonist:

- *puts a lot of work into many small images*

- *uses many drawings to show a scene*

- *makes art that is skimmed over fairly quickly*

- *draws his or her characters over and over again*

That's why comic art can be such simple art. It's repetitive, skippable, and can reveal its information a bit at a time—it doesn't need to happen all at once in a single picture.

So if you're not a great artist right now and can't draw much more than stick figures, that's fine. **Simple is great**. Many comic artists who can draw with lots of realistic detail draw more simply on purpose. Why draw all those details that people just skip over as they read?

You can tell complex or deep stories with simple art

As you grow up, you add a lot of words to your vocabulary. A child might say "red," but an older person might use "scarlet" or "crimson" to describe a specific kind of red. But Little Scarlet Riding Hood doesn't have the same ring to it, does it?

Now if you think about the things you draw the same way you think of words you learn, you can see that artists also add to their **visual vocabulary** over time.

As a child you might have drawn "sun" like this.

But a more experienced artist might draw "sun" like this.

Again, that doesn't mean the story with the second kind of sun will be better. After all, they both do kind of the same thing. They show you a sun.

You probably **can already draw** a lot of simple words. Cartoonist Scott McCloud calls these "icons." Most are based on a simple shape.

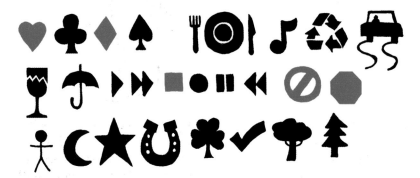

Anything you can identify from its **outline** can be an icon.

You may not have seen these icons on signs before, but can you tell what they are?

Icons connect

When you need to find a bathroom, even if you're in a foreign country, the same simple **stick figures** are there to guide you.

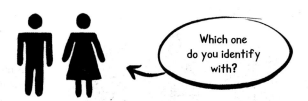

Which one do you identify with?

It doesn't matter if you're Superman or the Wolfman, Wonder Woman or the Bride of Frankenstein, you know which one speaks to you.

Now what about these two characters? Does either one seem like you? Probably not, because these two are specific people. They have details you might not share. But the generic bathroom icons can be any person. So if you draw a comic with simple icons as characters, more people will be able to relate them.

The most beloved cartoon characters are usually pretty simple. Spider-Man's mask hides the details of Peter Parker's face, letting us pretend we could be wearing it instead. Sure, he is more detailed than a stick figure, but the point is this: keeping things simple is a good place to start.

Shapes help identify characters

Since most stories have more than one character, the characters can't all be the same icon or stick figure. The difference between the washroom man and woman is the dress. The shape is different.

What if you wanted to draw specific monsters? You could still use washroom-like figures but **change their shape** a little bit.

You can still draw simply but make each of your characters look different by changing their shape.

Can you tell Dracula, the Wolfman, Frankenstein, and his bride apart?

Icons work not just for characters but also for **settings** (the time and place of your comic). The more simple the background, the more it can be imagined to be any place. The pictures on the right could be almost any forest in autumn or any house at night.

Icons as emoticons

Drawing emotions can be tricky because there are so many muscles on our faces to consider. Like how do your eyes squint when you make a big smile? Plus, the ways that people express themselves can be slightly different from person to person. Maybe your bored face looks like someone else's sad face?

Cartoonists sometimes use icons to show emotion when words won't do, or when a character (or the cartoonist) can't find the right words.

Without these icons, what these people are feeling might not be as clear. Maybe the last girl in the row below is just raising her hand to ask to use the bathroom!

Until you feel ready to draw subtle expressions, you can use shortcuts like these icons to help tell your story.

What's that smell?

You have five senses. Pictures show sight and texture. Sound effects and word balloons show sound. You can use words for smell and taste, but you can also use icons instead.

If you put some **wavy lines** and suggestive **icons** by something, they tell the reader that's what it smells like.

Without icons, wavy lines either mean steam or suggest something is stinky.

On the rare occasion you want to show taste without words, you just have the icon come from the taster's mouth or tongue.

Letters are icons, too

The letter "P" tells people where to park. An "H" means "hospital."

And these road signs are just letters, too, aren't they? The first one is a "T" and the second an "I" taking a break.

If you know how to print **letters** and **numbers**, you can already make all the lines you need to draw.

O is a circle.

0 is an oval.

C is an arc.

7 and **Z** are zigzags.

S is a squiggle.

I is a straight line.

L and **T** are straight lines meeting each other.

You can build simple shapes with all of these alphabetical and numerical lines.

Of course, you'll want to **hide the fact** you're using these shapes, or people will just see the numbers and letters. But as a cartoonist you'll know the secret that they're there.

You're already closer to drawing awesomely than you knew!

A FINAL THOUGHT:

Simple has worked for centuries

From cave drawings to emoticons, people have long used simple images to communicate and tell stories. Trying to draw "better" is a great goal to have. But clear and simple pictures will always do the trick.

ICONS
AND SHAPES

Time for you to have some fun with icons, shapes, and the alphabet!

1 a. Test your visual vocabulary by filling a page with as many icons as you can.

b. Look at your page—circle any icons you think indicate emotions.

Some, like hearts, will be obvious, but can you see any new ways to communicate a person's inner thoughts through your icons?

c. Draw three heads. Replace all the eyes with icons. What could your drawings possibly express?

2 a. Draw icons of four famous characters.

b. Now draw icons of yourself and three friends or family members.

3 **a.** Draw something that smells like something else.

b. Draw someone tasting something surprising.

4 **a.** Using letters and numbers, or parts of letters and numbers, draw a face, a building, an animal, and a food. Try to make the letters and numbers invisible to other people.

b. Now have a friend print some letters and numbers randomly on a few pages. Turn them into drawings that make the letters and numbers tricky to see.

PRO TIP

It's not cheating to erase. All professional artists use an eraser with pencil or correction fluid with ink.

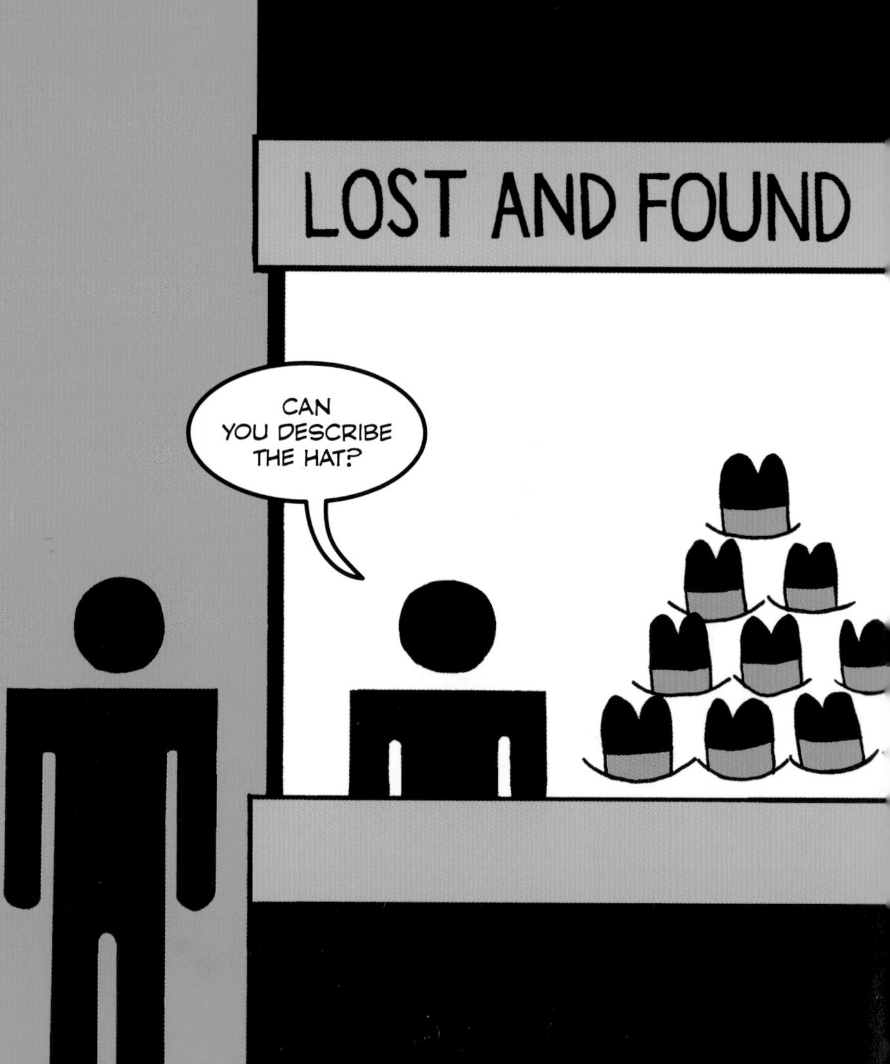
LOST AND FOUND
CAN YOU DESCRIBE THE HAT?

DETAILS MAKE *the* DIFFERENCE

When you can't show everything, you need to know how to choose the best details for your reader.

Photographs give us a complete picture—all the details. Icons give us the bare bones—the simplest way of showing something. Those are the two extremes. **In between them** is an area called "cartoony." Instead of having all the details or none of them, you have some of them. Which ones? Choosing wisely is essential because it's often the details that tell your reader what's important in a story.

So what *are* the important details?

When people say a drawing has lots of "detail," they usually mean it has a lot of little lines, like these.

...OUT THESE TINY SILVER SPOONS THAT HAVE BEEN ENGRAVED WITH THE SAME PATTERN OF MY AUNT JENNIFER'S CUTLERY. IT'S AN OVERLAPPING SWIRL. ANYWAY, I'M STILL WAITING FOR THIS AVOCADO ICE CREAM...

GET TO THE POINT!

But sometimes too many lines are just background noise—like extra words that make a story harder to follow.

What's most important in comics are story details, like these.

How do details work?

The reality is, you don't actually notice everything you see. You just get a **general impression**. How many hairs does your best friend have? It doesn't matter. Instead, you remember your friend's hair color and style.

So why would you need to draw every hair on a character's head? No one's going to notice it anyway. You could, if it's fun to draw. But it probably isn't going to make your comic any better.

You focus only on what's important at the time

We all ignore complex things sometimes. But we also ignore simple things, if they're not important at the time. When you look at a scene, you can't pay attention to all of it.

For instance, if you went to the bank to open an account, you might notice how the pens were attached to the counter. If you went there to rob it, you'd notice where the security cameras are.

The same is true for comics. You only need to put in the details that are **important for your story**.

Here are **two drawings** of the same kitchen. What do you think each comic would be about?

Shapes aren't always enough

We know that the shape of something can help describe an object (see the icons on page 36). But when different objects have the **same shape**—like these three rectangles—how can you tell them apart?

The power of details

Details are recognizable, even when the shape they're shown in is not. For example, Frankenstein usually has a rectangular head, but you can draw any shape as long as you include other signature details, like his haircut, neck bolts, and stitches.

And you don't need to use geometric shapes. You can take almost **any shape** and turn it into something else.

Stylish shapes

Now that you know you can use any shape, you can have some fun. The shapes you choose for your characters say a lot not just about who they are but who created them. They are part of your style.

If you look at famous cartoon characters, you can often recognize them just by their outline, or **silhouette** (pronounced sill-oh-et). Do these shapes remind you of any cartoon characters?

These are the **simple** shapes on which Lisa Simpson, Dora the Explorer, and Charlie Brown are based. Each cartoonist chose very different shapes to draw the children.

Think about how Batman has those pointy ears, or SpongeBob SquarePants is so square. **Memorable characters** often have memorable silhouettes. Maybe your main characters should, too?

Color is a detail

Color can be a detail, too. Just like the lines on the tree back on page 46, color can add lots of detail or just enough.

This book is mostly drawn in a "**modernist**" art style. Its simple artwork suits the simple secrets of the book. That's why full color hasn't been used a lot. There is just enough color to tell you what's going on and to keep your eyes interested.

But when should you use color?

Lots of amazing comics have been in **black and white**, like manga or older newspaper comics. If you decide you want to **add color**, the first items to color are the ones that help make your story clear.

Without color (or more words) you can't be sure if there's a love connection or not.

 Start by coloring everything that has to be a certain color to make your story clear. Think about what details need color to be clear, like whether a nose is bloody or runny. You can stop there, or...

Next, you can turn to the things that can be a number of colors. Here's your chance to add mood. Is the sky a romantic orange, a stormy grey, a calm blue? What season is it? These trees suggest these kids might be starting a new school year.

Finally, you can turn to the things that can be any color, like clothes, cars, books, etc. Pick colors that help make your story clear. For example, red bricks wouldn't make the boy's hair stand out enough.

Sketching

To learn what details and shapes to draw, you need to practice. That's what sketching is.

Some artists keep a **sketchbook**. Others prefer using scrap paper. Use whichever seems right to you. The important thing is to **draw regularly**— knowing what something looks like and knowing how to draw it are two different things. If you're having trouble drawing something, like hands, feet, cars, or whatever, go and look at the thing and sketch it. Draw it from different angles. Try different shapes and details.

The difference between doodling and sketching

Doodling is when you draw things you **already know** how to draw. Like what you draw in the margin of a notebook or while talking on the phone.

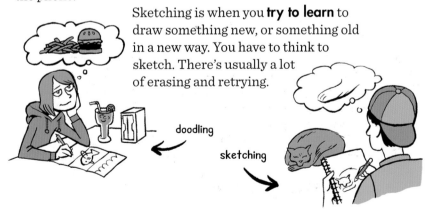

Sketching is when you **try to learn** to draw something new, or something old in a new way. You have to think to sketch. There's usually a lot of erasing and retrying.

doodling

sketching

Thumbnails

Cartoonists often sketch to plan a scene before they draw a final comic. These sketches are called **thumbnails** because they're drawn small. Sketching allows you to think "out loud" on paper, which is easier than picturing the drawings in your head. It's like the rough draft you do for your writing.

Here are some thumbnails for the rock 'n' roll animal comic that appears later on page 76.

A FINAL THOUGHT:

Practice makes awesome

Deciding which details to use and which to leave out is part of the art of making comics. If you sketch enough, you'll get better at putting the right details on the right shapes to make awesome comics.

DETAILS

Do you have an eye for detail yet?
These fun exercises will help develop your ability
to notice the small stuff.

1 a. Draw the outside of your home. Include the details that you'd use to tell a story about Santa or a burglar trying to get inside.

   b. Redraw your home for a story about playing hide-and-go-seek.

2 a. Draw your bedroom. Include the details for a story about a monster who likes to sleep among your clothes.

   b. Redraw your bedroom. Include details for a story about doing chores.

3 a. Draw three rectangles. Use details to turn them into an envelope, a magazine, and a box of cereal.

   b. Draw three circles. Turn them into a clock, a fruit, and a wheel.

4 a. Trace the shapes of ten comic characters. Can you tell who they are?

   b. Write a list of cartoon characters you could identify just from their silhouette.

5 Draw a circle, a triangle, an oval, and a rectangle. Turn them into a famous character's head or body. Repeat with two more characters. Here's a list in case you can't think of any off the top of your head.

- Super Mario or Princess Peach
- Cookie Monster or Miss Piggy
- Godzilla or King Kong
- Cowardly Lion or the Tin Man
- Wolverine or Storm

- Mr. Potato Head or Barbie
- Medusa or the Minotaur
- Blackbeard or Captain Hook
- Baby New Year or Cupid
- Mother Nature or Father Time

6 Make up six new characters and use the shape of objects to make them unique. You can get ideas from the list below.

- Food and drinks
- Vehicles
- Pets
- The farm
- Outer space
- Household objects
- Eating utensils
- Tools
- Sports
- Plants
- Buildings
- Music

PRO TIP

Cartoonists draw with pencil and trace their own drawings, fixing what is wrong. They might use tracing paper or a light table (that's a glass table with a light underneath). I used an erasable blue pencil for most of the art in this book. When scanners are set to "line art," they don't see the blue lines—only the lines that I want to keep get scanned into the computer.

7 Add a few details to simple stick figures to create four people you know. See if your friends can figure out who they are.

Draw four more stick figures and make them into famous people.

Draw four more and make them into comic characters.

8 Go back and look at some of your favorite artists and see how they simplified places and objects. Trace or copy six panels that have settings. See what you can learn from them.

9 Have a friend draw a bunch of shapes on a page. Turn each of them into a person, animal, or object.

10 Build your visual vocabulary this month. Figure out how to do a cartoony drawing of one object each day. Sketch the object while it sits in front of you, but simplify it enough that you can draw it from memory. You can start with simple things, like boxes and balls, and work your way up to more complex objects, like bicycles and vacuum cleaners.

11 Go to a public place and watch people. Fill two pages with sketches of different people. You might go to parks, shopping malls, city hall, the library, or anywhere else you think there will be lots of people. If you're shy, bring a friend along to chat with (and don't forget to get your parents' permission, too).

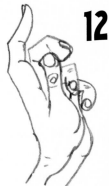

12 Sketch a page full of hands. Fill another page with feet and/or shoes. Pick an object you find a challenge to draw and create several on a page as well.

PRO TIP
Sketch from real life—it challenges you to understand depth and angles. If you always sketch a nose straight on, you won't be able to draw one when a character's head is turned to the side.

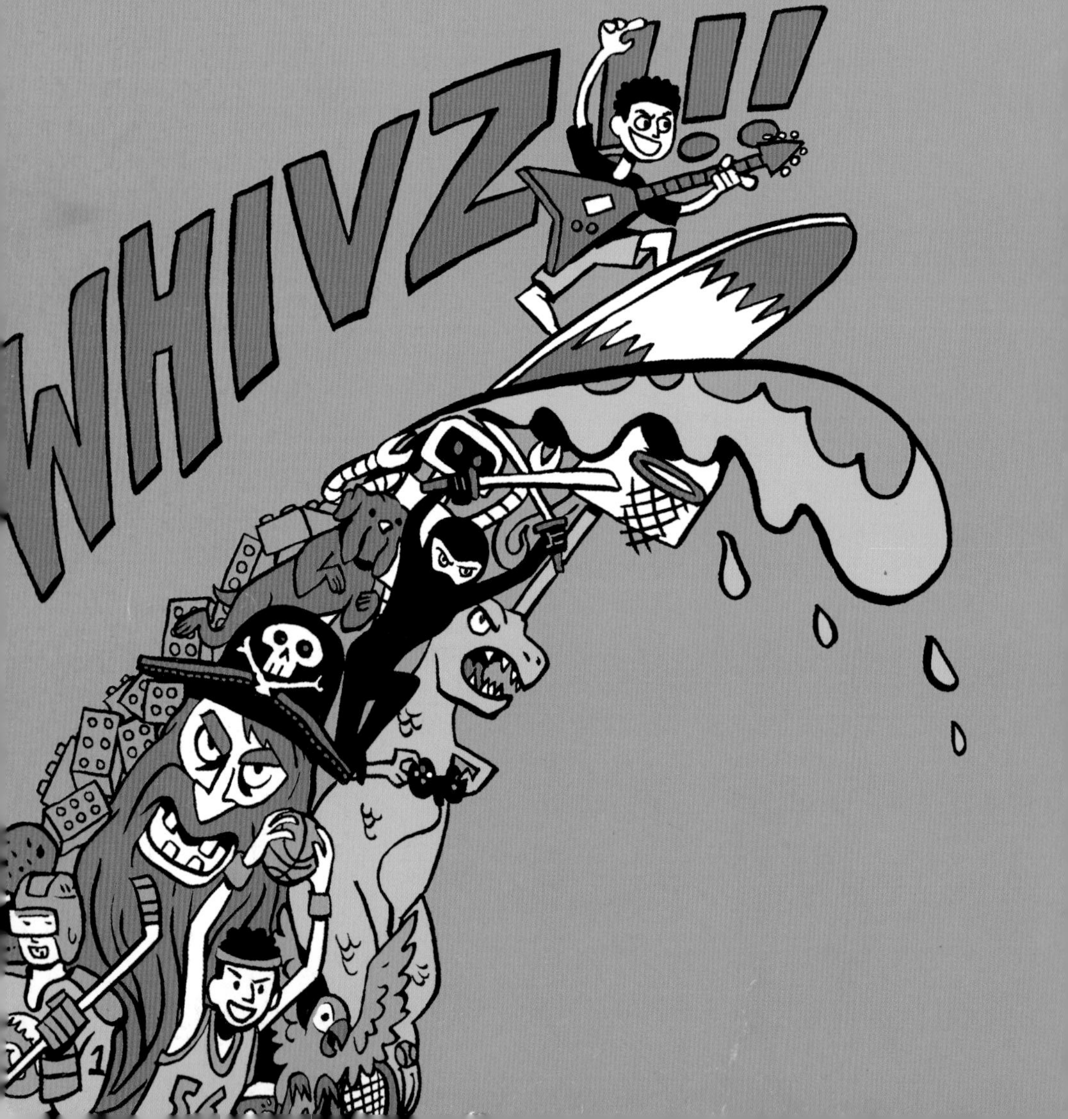
WHIVZ!!!

let the PERSONALITY SHINE

Learning how to use shapes and details is important to developing your own drawing style. But to really show off, you've gotta give your drawings personality.

Look at the lines below. If the lines were people, how would you describe their personalities?

Lines have character

When you're in a certain mood, your body reacts in a certain way. If you're nervous, you might shake. If you're angry, you probably tense up. What kinds of lines would you draw if you felt those emotions? Use lines to help you **communicate** your characters' feelings.

Drawing is your chance to be an **actor**. Choose an emotion and pretend you are feeling it as you draw someone with that same emotion. See how your drawing changes. You may find yourself making faces as you go!

Giving your characters character

A personality is all about a character's typical emotions and behavior. Is she patient? Grumpy? Silly? Fidgety? Drawing these things can be tough, but there are a few tricks you can use to help tell people what your character is like and how she feels about something.

Body language

You can probably draw a happy face and a frowny face. But can you draw a happy body and an unhappy body? Even stick figures can be bent and folded to **show their reactions**. These poses aren't hard to draw, though they might take time to think of.

Here are a bunch of characters who've just received bad news.

Drawing a black shadow under characters can show that they have weight. And when they jump in the air, a shadow can show how high they're jumping.

The "magic if"

Once, a theater director with the awesome name of Constantin Stanislavski came up with the idea of the "**magic if**." To help actors improve their performances, he asked them to imagine **what would happen if** they were in certain situations.

You can use the "magic if" to force yourself to think like an actor and figure out what makes each of your characters **different**. What would they do if they won the lottery? Got fired? Joined a soccer league? Grew another head?

Here are a bunch of different characters who have found a lost wallet.

So how do your characters react to good news? Does one cry with joy, another give out high-fives, and yet another take photos to share later? By asking these questions, you can learn more about who your characters are...which makes them easier to draw and use in your stories.

Comic costumes

Personality is not just about emotional reactions or body posture—clothes also say something about a character's personality, since what we wear is part of our behavior.

Someone's whole personality can't be summed up by what he or she wears, but a cartoonist can use clothing to give **clues** to a character's identity. Who are these people?

You'd probably say a doctor and a burglar. If you wanted to be a doctor or a burglar for Halloween, you'd probably dress in those clothes, too. So costumes are clothes that quickly tell you about someone's identity.

Does every doctor and burglar dress like that? No. But if you draw these characters with these clothes, it gives your reader a quick clue about who they are.

Which approach is easier to understand?

In a long graphic novel, you would have the time and space to make a more realistic doctor and burglar—ones that didn't wear such obvious costumes. But in a shorter comic you often don't have that kind of time. You need to get to the point! Costumes are very useful here.

Costumes aren't always fair, but they work. People think nerds wear glasses. I'm a nerd and I wear glasses, but lots of nerds don't wear glasses, and lots of people with glasses are super cool. Still, if you add some glasses to a cartoon character, people will think that person's supposed to be brainy. Oh well.

Costumes involve more than clothing. They can also include **props that reveal** personality. What do these props tell you about these characters' personalities?

Together, props and costumes give clues to a character's job or home. They work so well, you can even add them to well-known characters, such as these monsters.

65

Sound effects

Sound effects are another personality-adding tool. They don't just show sound—they also show how you hear sound. There's a fancy word for this called **onomatopoeia** (pronounced on-o-mah-toe-pea-uh). That's when you use a made-up word to indicate a sound.

What words would you use for a drum set falling down a flight of stairs? **BADOOMBA BUMP A DUMPA CRASH!** might sound good to you. Or maybe **THUMP! THUMP! CONK! BONK! DONK!** Or simply **CRASH!**

Because we all **imagine sounds differently**, this is a chance for you to show some of your own personality.

Why should you use sound effects?

You could draw a silent explosion and let the reader imagine the sound, but a **BOOM!** adds more energy.

Here's a great place to use the lines with personality! Your lettering can also help show how a sound sounds.

Dress up your setting

Do you enjoy drawing characters, but don't like settings as much? Try to think of the **setting as a person**. How can you show that a place has a character of its own?

Here are a few different bedrooms with personality. What can you guess about the people who live in each one?

A FINAL THOUGHT:
Comics are about people

With comics you get to share your life and the lives of the people you know (real or fictional) with others. Putting personality into your comic lets people get to know you without even having to meet you.

EMOTIONS AND SOUNDS

Come on out! It's time for your personality to take center stage with pencil and paper.

1 Choose an emotion, then try to feel it. Make some lines that express what you feel (try closing your eyes). Use those lines to show a person expressing that same emotion.

2 Go back to the work of your favorite artists and trace one character showing at least four different expressions.

3 In front of a mirror, act out a variety of emotions. Look at how you use your body to express them. Draw five of these body poses— drawing either yourself or a favorite character. Think: does that character feel emotions (such as sadness or happiness) the same way you do?

4 Go someplace where there is lots of noise. Close your eyes and try to come up with sound effects for at least five noises you hear around you. Draw them in a comic panel.

5 Make a list of as many costumes as you can think of. Draw at least ten of them.

6 a. Draw a one-panel comic about a character discovering a wallet. Use the list of characters from page 55 if you want.

b. Draw the same comic but add a second character. How do the two characters interact with each another?

7 a. Make up three onomatopoeic examples for each of the groups below.

- *Animal sounds*
- *Weather sounds*
- *Mechanical noises*
- *Sports sounds*
- *Human voice (nonverbal)*
- *Construction noises*

b. Choose nine of them and draw them as sound effects.

8 Draw the characters you think might live in each of the bedrooms on page 67.

9 Imagine five unique settings of your own. Then think of characters that might fit in each setting. The characters could live there, be trying to find it, or even be trying to escape from it. Pick one setting and character and draw them.

10 Pick four fictional characters. Draw each character's favorite vehicle, his favorite chair, and his recreational room. See if your friends can figure out who each item belongs to without any hints.

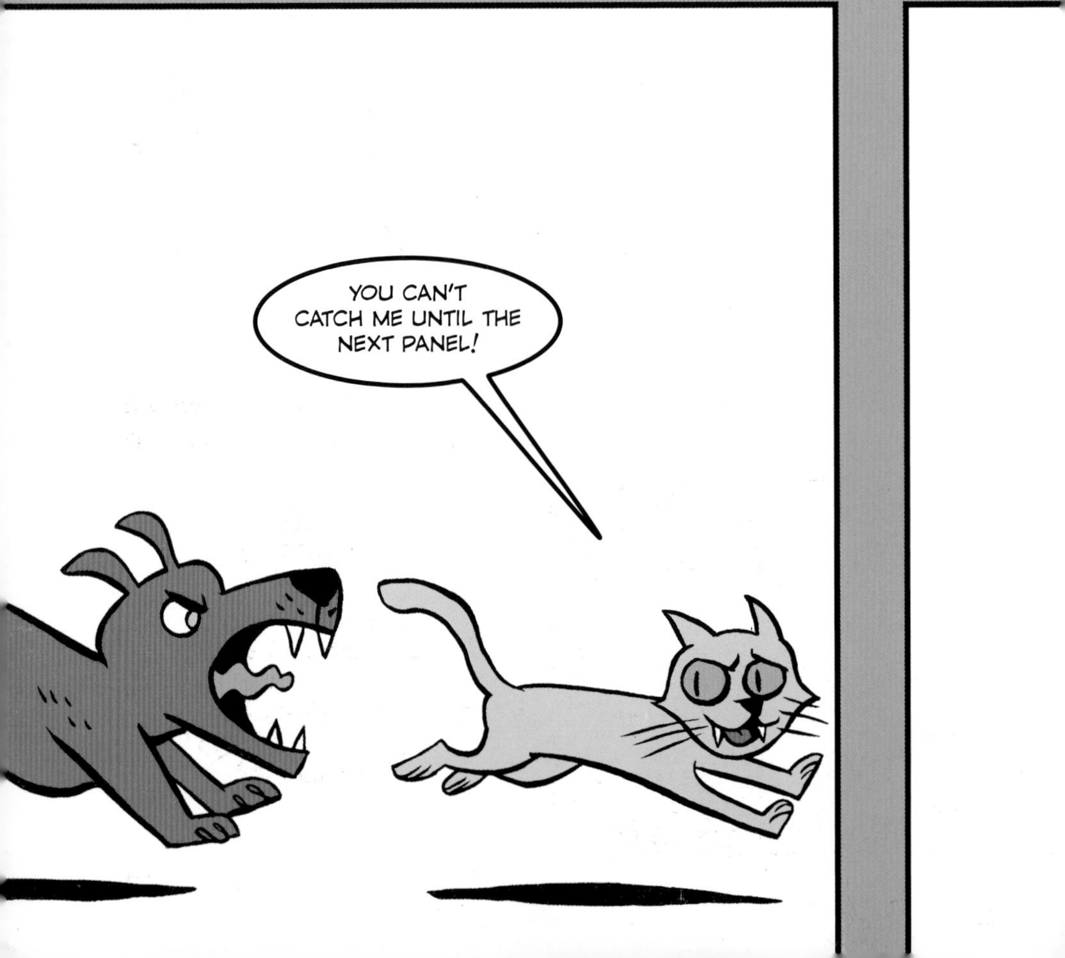
YOU CAN'T CATCH ME UNTIL THE NEXT PANEL!

TAKE IT ONE MOMENT at a TIME

SECRET Six

Each panel in your comic shows a moment in time. When you put the panels together, you build a story.

Your comic needs as many panels as you feel there are important **moments** to share with your reader. But what is a moment? How long does one last?

Well, sometimes a moment is only a split second frozen in time, like a snapshot from a photograph.

But **comics isn't photography**. And a panel can show much more than a split second. For example, by adding words you add extra time to each panel. After all, a word balloon shows sound, and sound takes time to happen. Your moment isn't a split second anymore.

I have to mention Scott McCloud again here. His book *Understanding Comics* has a lot of great points I'm building on for this chapter.

In fact, most of comics grammar (such as word balloons, sound effects, and motion lines) **expands the split second** of a panel's image into a longer moment. The length of the moment even depends on how fast you read the panel compared to the next person.

Look at the three panels below and think about how much time might be passing in each one.

Give me a moment

In real life, a moment could last anywhere from a second to over a minute. The word "moment" gives us some **wiggle room**. "I'll be back in a moment" is spoiled if you have to give an exact time, like "I'll be back from the washroom in three minutes and eight seconds." Time doesn't need to be measured exactly.

Written vs. drawn moments

What seems like a single moment in writing might not be a single moment in a drawing. Why? Because the number of moments change depending on if you're trying to show actions over time or describing something.

You could write a sentence full of actions, like "I got dressed, brushed my teeth, had breakfast, and went to school." That takes only a second or two to read, but in a comic it has four different locations and four different actions. See?

Are all these moments **important to the story**? If it's about going to school, you might skip right to the character at a bus stop. If it's about a trip to the dentist, brushing teeth might be important. You can choose based on your story.

But what if the words that you were trying to draw were like this?

> She wore shiny star-shaped earrings, an elegant gown, and a tiara with a heart among swirling silver. Her long red hair fell in a tangle like jellyfish tendrils on either side of her large, light blue eyes. I knew at once that she was a princess.

That's a lot of words, and yet you could draw them **all in one image**. That's because they're all descriptions, not actions

Details or time?

The key is to know which words are **descriptive details** (easy to show in one drawing) and which words are **action details** (hard to show in one drawing). It's up to you to select the right moments for your panels.

KEEPING ORDER

When you read a panel, you generally go from left to right, like when you read regular books. Something happens on the left side that the right side reacts to. See how it can be awkward if we put the reaction on the left instead of the right?

WHO'S THERE?

KNOCK, KNOCK!

Gutter time

The space between panels is called the gutter. That's where the reader **imagines the story**. The time inside one panel is a brief moment, but the time between panels can be anything from a millisecond to millions of years. Your clues help the reader fill in the blanks of the gutters.

Each example starts at the same moment but **skips over** a different span of time, depending on the story. The first one is about waiting. The second one is about the party. The third one is about disappointment.

Panel speed

How quickly you read a comic panel has a lot to do with its size—smaller panels tend to go by quickly, whereas larger panels go by more slowly.

Of course, this idea assumes that the panels have a similar amount of stuff in them. You'll spend more time looking at a panel packed with images or words than you will an emptier one.

Which of these panels do you spend the most time on?

WITH MY SUPER EARS, I CAN HEAR THE ALARM GOING OFF AT THE BLOOD BANK. I BET DR. DRACULA AND THE FANG BANGERS ARE UP TO THEIR OLD TRICKS. TIME TO SAVE THE DAY AS THE CERULEAN STREAK!

You spent less time reading the final panel, didn't you? The first two panels may have been smaller, but they had more information in them.

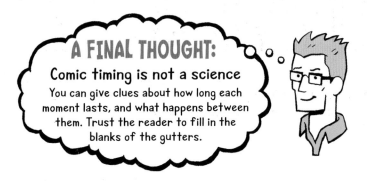

A FINAL THOUGHT:

Comic timing is not a science

You can give clues about how long each moment lasts, and what happens between them. Trust the reader to fill in the blanks of the gutters.

TIMING AND ORDER

This is your moment to live in the moment.
Time's ticking! Let's get to it!

1 a. Cut up a sheet of paper into four pieces of the same size. On one piece of paper, draw the first panel of a comic. If you need an idea, choose a line of dialogue from the list below.

- "Are you hungry?"
- "I've been thinking about growing a beard."
- "You're never going to get me to wear that hat!"

- "Will you help me find my lost dog?"
- "Run, it's a monster!"
- "What do you want for the second scoop of ice cream?"

b. On a second piece of paper, draw another panel showing that only a little time has passed.

c. On another piece of paper, draw a different panel showing that a lot of time has passed.

d. On your fourth piece, add a panel that takes place before the start of the comic. It can be a long or short time before. If you like, try adding more new panels to the beginning or end of the comic.

2 Pick one of the lists below and draw the events using as few panels as possible. You choose when to use pictures or words to tell the reader what is happening.

a. You had two tickets to a concert.
You gave one to your friend.
You both took the bus to the concert.
You got a concert shirt.
The band played your favorite song.
You sang along.
After the show you lost your voice.
You didn't lose your bus fare.
You took the bus home with your friend.

b. Frankenstein was in a graveyard.
Dracula showed up.
He had a picnic basket.
They ate worm sandwiches.
They sat on a checkered blanket.
Ants showed up.
Frankenstein was sad that ants were ruining their picnic.
Dracula didn't agree.
He ate the ants. Mmmmm!

c. A girl found a note in her locker.
She read it. It said, "You have the nicest hair. Your Secret Admirer."
She looked around the hallway at classmates and wondered who sent it.
Billy? Jin? Sanjay?
She went to the bathroom, looked in the mirror, and smiled as she brushed her hair.
She thought, "This is the best secret since my surprise party!"

> ### PRO TIP
> Cartoonists draw their images **much** larger than they appear in a book. I draw things about 1.5 to 2 times as big as what you see in print. The art is then reduced by the computer, which makes it appear tighter and more detailed. Doing the opposite (working small and making it bigger) will make work appear fuzzier and messier.

3 Draw a chase scene using at least six panels.

Use panels of different sizes to see how they affect the speed of the chase. Then redraw the same comic with different panels to see if you can change the speed at with which the chase is read.

Maybe it starts fast and ends slow?

Maybe it starts slow and ends fast?

Maybe obstacles slow down the action in the middle?

Some ideas for a chase:

- *Policeman trying to catch a pickpocket*
- *Two people running a marathon*
- *Parent chasing after a toddler*
- *Motorcycle chasing a car*
- *Fox chasing a rabbit*
- *Rabbit chasing a talking carrot*
- *Fan chasing a rock star*
- *Shark chasing a fish*
- *Lightbulb chasing a lamp*
- *Beaver chasing a peg-legged pirate*

PRO TIP

When making the borders of your panels, use a T-square for a straighter line. A T-square is like a ruler but with an anchor on the side that pushes against the edge of the paper to keep it straight.

You can also use a T-square to make guidelines for your text so the words are on straight lines. After cartoonists write over the words with ink, they erase the pencil lines.

4 One great way to play with your panel speed is to show a quick closeup of an action connected to the story. Draw five panels, each with one of the actions from the list below. Use motion lines to show what's happening. Feel free to add a sound effect.

- Hammering something
- Using a salt shaker
- Using a yo-yo
- Flicking a switch
- Throwing something
- Catching a thrown item
- Dropping a rock
- Bouncing on a trampoline
- Rearranging knickknacks
- Doing push-ups
- Snapping a twig
- Scratching an itch

PRO TIP
Motion lines show the direction in which something or someone has moved in a moment. They often go from thick to thin as they move forward in time. To suggest something is shaking, add lines around the object that mirror its outline.

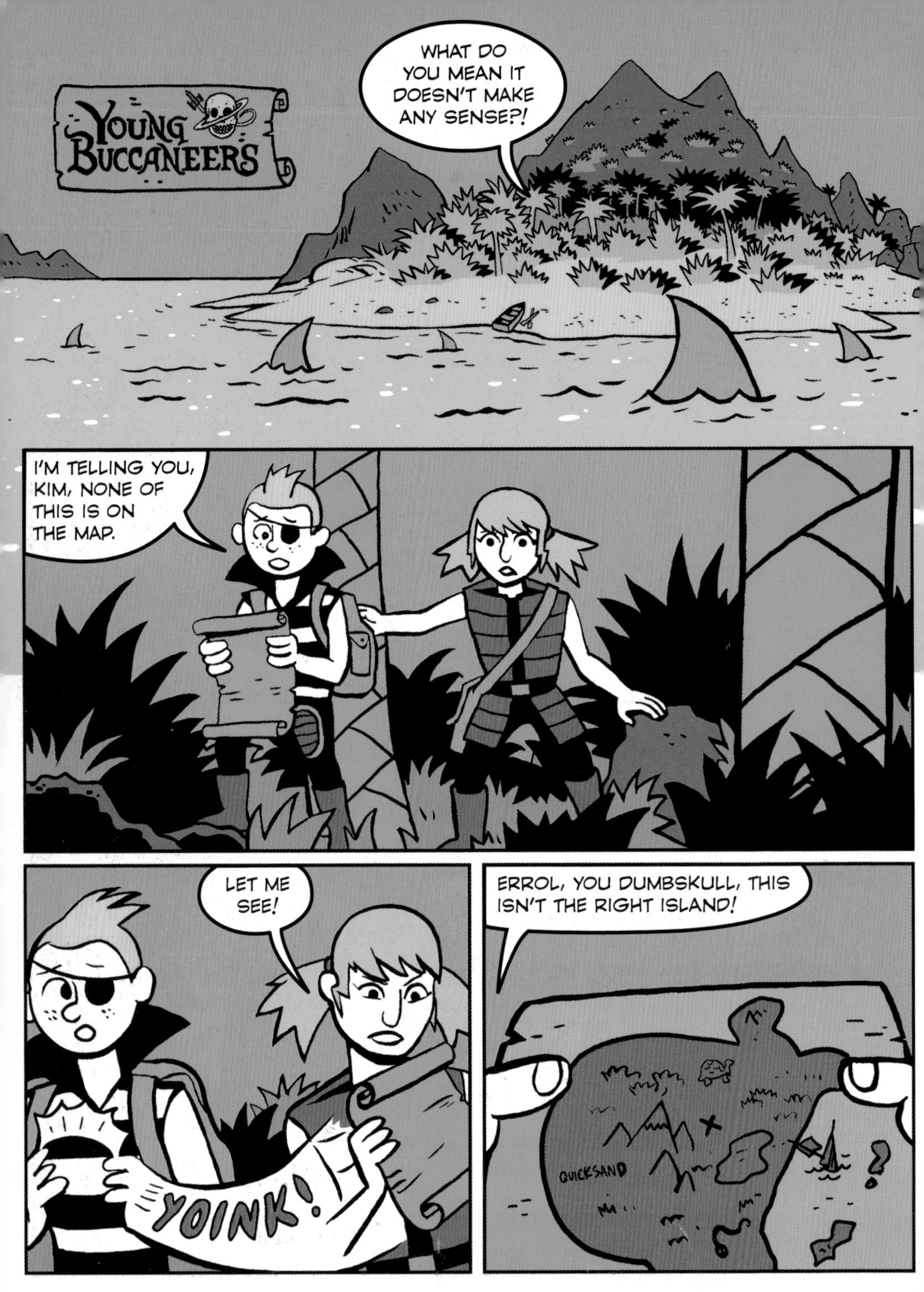
YOUNG BUCCANEERS
WHAT DO YOU MEAN IT DOESN'T MAKE ANY SENSE?!
I'M TELLING YOU, KIM, NONE OF THIS IS ON THE MAP.
LET ME SEE!
YOINK!
ERROL, YOU DUMBSKULL, THIS ISN'T THE RIGHT ISLAND!
QUICKSAND

WHAT? BUT YOU OVERHEARD STARBEARD SAY...

...DROID ISLAND IS WHERE THE TREASURE IS, I KNOW.

BUT THIS ISN'T A MAP OF DROID ISLAND. ARE YOU SURE YOU STOLE THE RIGHT ONE?

THERE'S MORE THAN ONE MAP? IF WE'VE GOT THE WRONG ONE, THEN WE'LL NEVER BEAT THEM TO THE TREASURE AND PROVE WE'RE REAL PIRATES.

I CAN STILL HEAR THE CAPTAIN'S INSULTS.

YE BE BUT TINY MINNOWS, NOT TRUE SHARKS LIKE WE.

WE'VE GOT TO PROVE HIM WRONG. WE HAVE TO SHOW HIM WE'RE NOT LITTLE KIDS. THERE'S TREASURE ON THIS ISLAND SOMEWHERE.

AYE. LET'S KEEP LOOKING.

I HOPE BARRY DOESN'T GET IN TROUBLE FOR HELPING US.

I WON'T TELL YOU WHERE THEY WENT! I MADE A TRUE PROMISE TO ERROL AND KIM. WE EVEN CROSSED CUTLASSES ON IT, LIKE REAL PIRATES. THERE'S NO WAY I'LL EVER TELL. JUST FORGET IT. NEVER EVER NOT A PEEP. NOT EVEN IN A GIGAZILLION BILLION YEARS!

WELL IF YE BE TOO THICKHEADED TO FEAR DAVY JONES' LOCKER, PER'APS YE WILL RESPOND TO DAVY JONES' PANTRY.

IF YE TALK, I'LL GIVE YE THIS PLATE OF MOUTHWATERIN' CRAB CAKES.

THEY TOOK A BOAT TO DROID ISLAND TO BEAT YOU TO THE TREASURE!

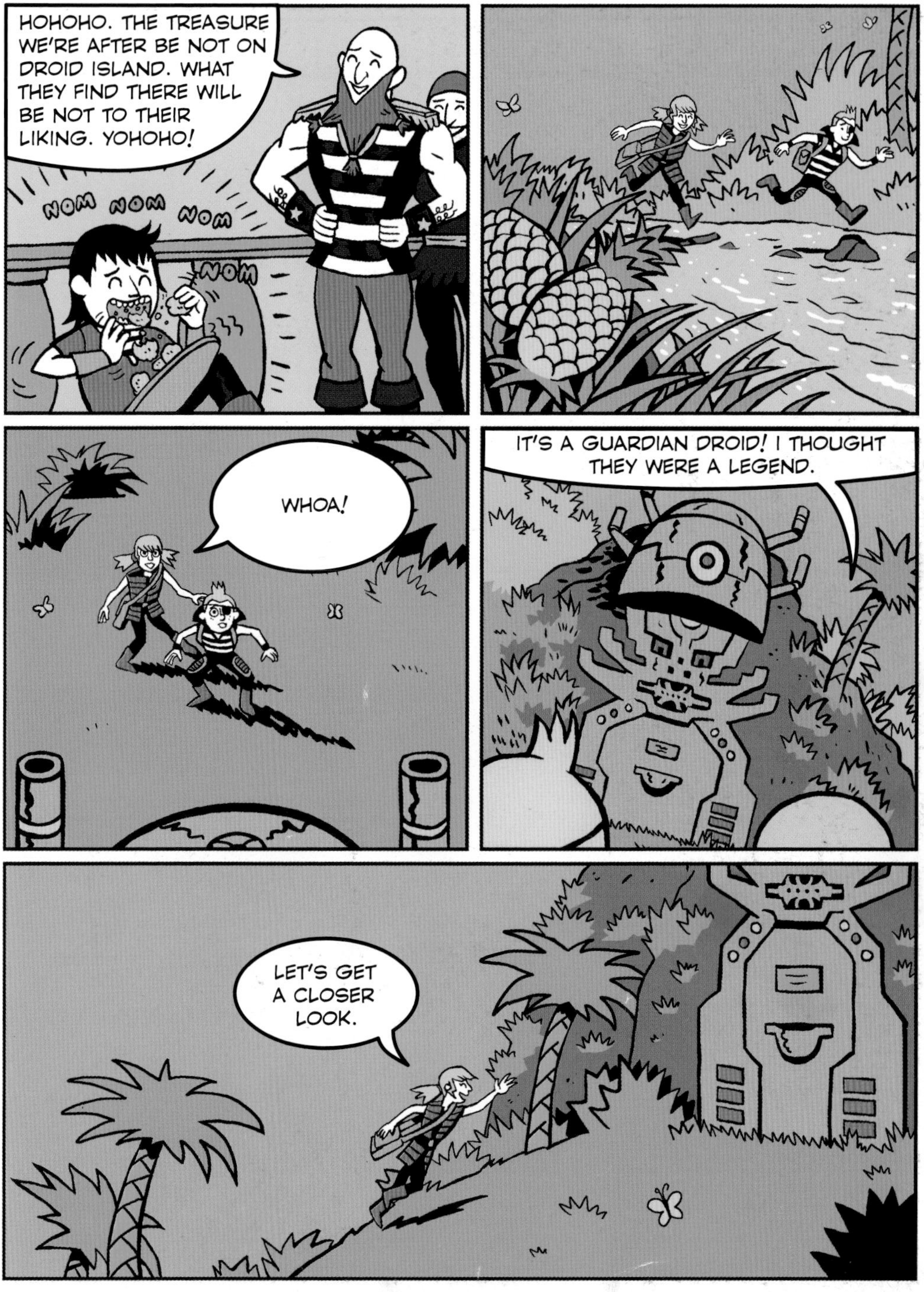
HOHOHO. THE TREASURE WE'RE AFTER BE NOT ON DROID ISLAND. WHAT THEY FIND THERE WILL BE NOT TO THEIR LIKING. YOHOHO!
NOM NOM NOM
NOM
WHOA!
IT'S A GUARDIAN DROID! I THOUGHT THEY WERE A LEGEND.
LET'S GET A CLOSER LOOK.

BUT...

YOU'RE SO BRAVE, MR. GROWN-UP PIRATE.

THERE'S A RIDDLE.

I HAVE A CROWN BUT I'M NOT ROYALTY. I HAVE SCALES BUT I'M NOT FISH OR LIZARD.

WHO HAS CLOWNS BESIDES ROYALTY? A CIRCUS, OF COURSE!

TAKE OFF THAT SILLY EYEPATCH—IT SAYS CROWN!

OH.

HOROSCOPES HAVE A SCALE, BUT NO CROWN.

THIS COULD TAKE A WHILE.

I'M GETTING HUNGRY. LET'S PICK SOME FRUIT.

THAT'S IT!

?

A PINEAPPLE HAS A CROWN AND SCALES!

THUNK!

CORRECT.

CLICK!

WHRRR!

WHOOSH!

SEE? WE'RE GROWN-UP TREASURE HUNTERS!

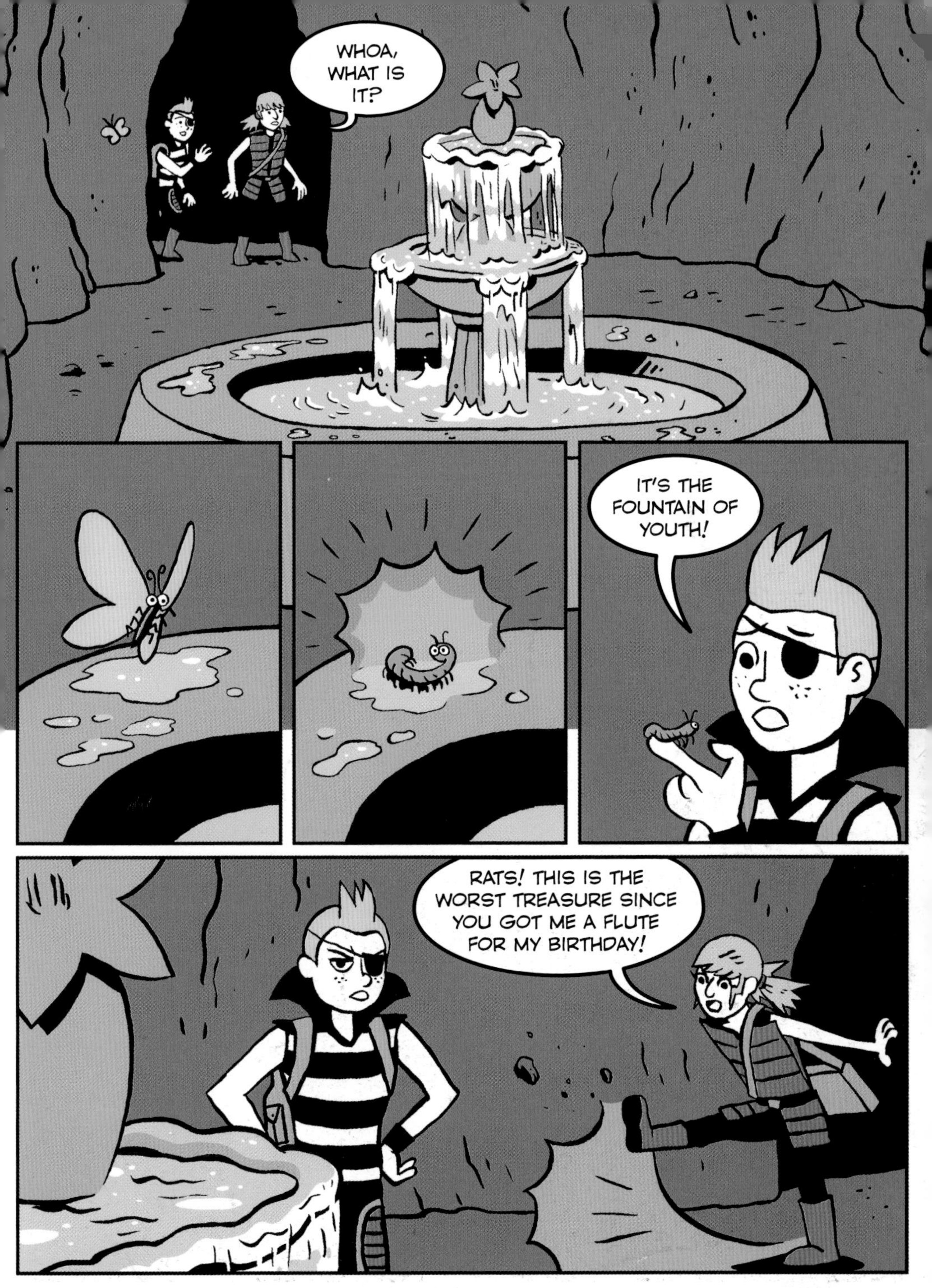
WHOA, WHAT IS IT?
IT'S THE FOUNTAIN OF YOUTH!
RATS! THIS IS THE WORST TREASURE SINCE YOU GOT ME A FLUTE FOR MY BIRTHDAY!

Definitions of tools that rule

Each definition below uses an example from the previous comic, but many of these techniques are used more than once. Reread the comic to see if you can find the others.

Establishing shot:
Changing locations? Use this to show your readers a new setting. After you've established the location, you don't have to show the full view and can just focus on what's important in each moment.

Full-body shot:
When a new character (or outfit) is introduced, show the person from head to toe. It's also good to give a full-body shot to show actions like standing defiantly, tiptoeing, climbing, or jumping.

Medium shot:
This shows your characters from the waist up. Useful for when the characters are holding props or making gestures.

Closeup:
During a conversation, you look at people's faces, so sometimes a face is all you need to draw.

Extreme closeup:
Get in close to a body part to see an intense emotion, like a screaming mouth, or a key moment, like fingers crossed behind a back for a lie.

Subject:
Sometimes your readers need to see something in detail. If people are discussing an important item, show that thing.

Transition:
Stories can jump back and forth, or transition, between different characters to show the exciting bits. Smooth transitions often mention which character the comic is about to switch to, such as: "I wonder how so-and-so is doing?"

I HAVE A CROWN BUT I'M NOT ROYALTY. I HAVE SCALES BUT I'M NOT FISH OR LIZARD.

Foreshadowing:
This drops a hint with words or pictures about something that will be important later. The pineapple in this panel gives a clue to the riddle's answer.

In media res:
Readers don't need to be told everything at the beginning. You can start comics *in media res*, which means "in the middle of things." Notice how later dialogue then helps the reader catch up on the story.

Cutaways:
Instead of always showing the main action and characters, show something else in the setting. This can suggest a mood or give more information. A silent cutaway panel is a great way to show time passing, too.

Circular panel:
Like a spotlight, this highlights an important moment or detail. It often shows a small detail from a more complete drawing nearby.

93

Flashback:
Some cartoonists use cloud-shaped panels to suggest that something happened in the past. Others prefer to use different colors (or black and white) to show an earlier moment in time.

P.O.V.:
It stands for Point of View. It puts us in the character's shoes (or in this case, the guardian droid's). Drawing this can be a challenge—it can show unusual perspectives, such as from high above.

Silent panel:
Showing silence using words is hard, but with silent panels, the moment can go on and on. You can use more than one in a row or use bigger silent panels to show a longer pause.

Foreground, middleground, background:
Overlap characters, settings, and props to show depth. Remember that the closer something is, the larger it will appear.

Tall rectangle panel:
These focus on a narrow moment of action, like a beanstalk growing or someone climbing a ladder.

Wide rectangle panel:
These focus on a wide moment, like a large landscape or someone running toward something.

94

Mechanical voice word balloon:

Use a squarish word balloon with a lightning bolt tail if technology is talking, like a TV or a robot. In a phone conversation, use it to show the person on the other end talking.

Chatterbox word balloon:

If you cram a balloon full of words, it's like the person won't shut up or is talking too fast. It also suggests that the other characters aren't even paying attention to the speaker.

Whisper word balloon:

A word balloon with a dotted outline shows a whisper. Because the line isn't solid, it suggests the words aren't quite there.

Drippy word balloon:

Use this for two reasons. One is for sarcasm, as in this comic. The other is to hint that the speaker is sick or gross—a pile of barf might talk in drippy word balloons.

Understated word balloon:

Leave a lot of space around a word (or words) to show something said quietly with a long pause surrounding it. It can capture a moment of great awe, weakness, shyness, or sadness.

A FINAL THOUGHT:

Cartoonists have a toolbox

Depending on what you're building, you'll use certain tools more often than others. Sometimes you can use a wrench to drive in a nail instead of a hammer. Think about your options before deciding to use the same old tool over and over again. You might build yourself a stronger story.

YOUR TURN

USING TOOLS

Now that you know a bunch of the tools that cartoonists use, let's build some awesome stuff!

1 Pick a fairy tale that starts with "Once upon a time..." or "There once was..." Draw a four-page version that starts *in media res*. Think about what other tools will help you tell the story. Like Goldilocks, find the one that's just right!

2 Draw six individual panels that each show something that happened to you in the past week. Use at least one different tool in each, such as a whisper, a flashback, a wide rectangle panel, etc. Think about how you can use panels to record your life.

PRO TIP: Kissing is bad. Not smooching, but the artist term "kissing." That's when two objects touch each other because of sloppy drawing. Objects should either have space between them or overlap. Otherwise, there's weird tension. Can you spot all the kisses?

3 Choose a page from a book you've read. Draw the comic version. Leave in the words you want, and draw what you can show with pictures instead of words. Try it again with three other books.

4 Draw a comic with some silent panels to show time passing. What size and shape panels do you use? How does the size affect the pacing? Some ideas for stories could be:

- Choosing what to get from the fridge
- Getting up the courage to ask someone to dance
- Waiting to use the bathroom
- Hiding from a monster
- Playing a video game
- Going for a hike
- Expecting an important phone call

5 a. From your favorite cartoonist's work, trace five panels that show foreground, middleground, and background.

   b. Draw five places from your life that have a foreground, middleground, and background. You can move around the spaces, turning the foreground into the background and vice versa.

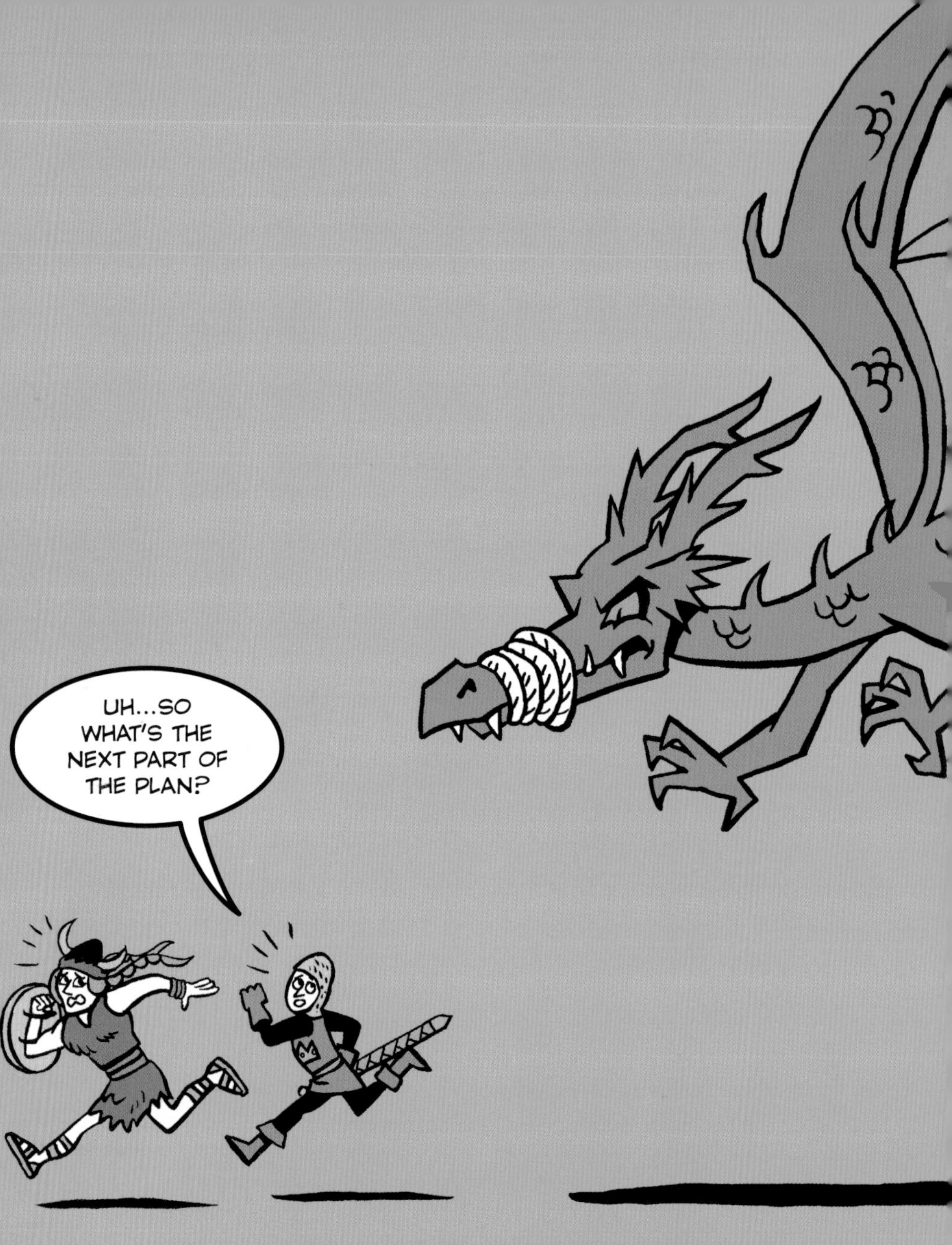
UH...SO WHAT'S THE NEXT PART OF THE PLAN?

YOU NEED
more
than ONE
GOOD
IDEA

SECRET
EiGHT

Now that you've learned about how to make comics, you might be wondering...how do you come up with a story?

Many people have a great idea for a comic—that first idea is your story's inspiration.

You can be **inspired by anything**. You may want to make a comic about a character from a novel. Or you may be inspired to write a story after hearing a song. Or you may be excited to try out a new art utensil or fun new comic format. There's no wrong place to begin.

Coming up with the rest

The hard part comes after the inspiration. You still need a lot more ideas to turn that inspiration into a **full story**. The following techniques can help you come up with lots of idea.

One of the most successful authors today is J. K. Rowling. Some people would say she had one idea: the Harry Potter books. But her stories aren't just about a boy who goes to a school for wizards. There are thousands more ideas—they also have Hermoine, Luna, Hogwart's, Diagon Alley, gillyweed, Bertie Bott's Every Flavor Beans, and tons more. **Blending these ideas** together took lots of thinking.

Sound intimidating? The good news is there are plenty of ways to come up with new ideas. Just as you can learn to draw and write, you can learn to imagine.

Say what?

A great way to get ideas is to overhear things. You might hear a snippet of a conversation on a bus, on a street corner, or at the mall that really catches your ear. Write it down and make up the rest. Who are these people, and what is the context for this weird conversation? Try using the "magic if" (see page 62) to help fill in the blanks.

In fact, applying the "magic if" technique to a character is a really great way to come up with new stories.

For writing comedy, mishearing, misspeaking, misreading, or misunderstanding things is even better. **Mistakes are great opportunities**. For instance, once when I was trying to say "sorceress," I got tongue-tied and said"swordceress" instead. Soon enough I had made a character for my Princess Planet comic who used swords instead of wands to cast her spells.

Write it down

Most people actually have lots of ideas, but they either fail to notice them or forget them. Try to **get in the habit** of writing down your ideas, good or bad. Don't worry about whether your ideas work for your comics. If you get in the habit of recording your ideas, you'll be able to pick and choose the best ones later on.

As you get more ideas, you can start to add them to specific lists, such as the ones shown below (of course, you can make different lists based on the type of story you want to tell). Then you can easily skim through what ideas you've come up with.

You might do something like this...

Objects that break in an action scene:	Motives for crimes:	Where dragons could live:
• Aquariums	• Revenge	• Dungeon
• Feather pillows	• Jealousy	• Swamp
• Ice sculptures	• Accident	• Waterfall
• Wax statues	• On a dare	• Volcano
• China shops	• Tradition	• Clouds

Sometimes coming up with ideas is just about combining two or more things that haven't been put together before...or at least not in that way. That's why we brainstorm ideas.

Making your brainstorm rain right

Brainstorming is the act of **quickly making lists** of things as they pop into your head. If you use categories for those things, it can help push you to think up better ideas.

First, pick a topic you want to draw a cartoon about. It might be part of longer story you're stuck on, or it might be for one short comic. Let's use "wizard" as an example.

Once you know your topic, make as long a list as you can under these five categories: living things, objects, actions, settings, and phrases. Then make a list of opposites for the first four categories (it's hard to come up with opposites for phrases). The contrast can spark even more ideas.

LIVING THINGS
Mumfred the Magician
Harry Potter
Merlin Gandalf sorcerer
warlock
spellcaster apprentice
witch
owl   scientist
cat   warrior
rat   peasant
familiar

OBJECTS
potion
wand
spellbook
staff
cauldron
robes
hat
long white beard
telescope
crystal ball
skulls   electric guitars
candles   shorts
grimoire   vacuum cleaner
ouija board
magic

ACTIONS
spellcasting
spelling
spellchecking
casting
fly casting
brewing
          surfing
          high-fiving
          playing football

PHRASES
Computer whiz
wizard of words
The Apprentice's "You're fired!"
Abracadabra
Alakazam
Alapeanutbuttersandwiches
Which witch is which?
a good medium is rare
I can spell that backwards

SETTINGS
Oz tower
castle
dungeon
library
séance
Hogwarts   beach
spelling bee   bowling alley
Halloween   high noon
witching hour

The word "spell" shows up a lot on the brainstorming
list, which could inspire this comic...

PASS ME MY
SPELLBOOK.

I DON'T WANT
A BOOK
FOR SPELLING
WORDS. I WANT
MY GRIMOIRE.

WHAT'S A
GRIMOIRE?

IT'S ANOTHER
WORD FOR
SPELLBOOK.

I WOULD HAVE
KNOWN THAT IF YOU
HAD LET ME GET THE
DICTIONARY.

...and the opposite
setting of "beach" led
to this gag.

After all, what if
a wizard DID go to
the beach?

Brainstorm doodles

Since comics are about drawing, you can also brainstorm with **doodles instead** of words. Remember from page 52 that doodling is drawing things you already know how to draw. (This is a great place to draw those icons you learned earlier, too.) Pick a topic and let your mind wander.

Draw as many doodles as you can that relate to one theme and look for connections. You should try to draw opposites again, too, because the conflict between the two can be interesting. Here are some doodles for wizards...

...and here are the comics they inspired.

Learning the tropes

A lot of stories use the same **basic elements**. These are called **tropes**. If you know the tropes of your comic's genre, you can use them...or break away from them and come up with a brand-new story.

For example, here are some tropes from fantasy-adventure stories:

- *A kid discovers her real parents were special, magical, or alien beings, and she has untapped special powers*

- *A kid discovers he is the chosen one of whom the prophecy speaks*

- *An old house has a secret portal hidden in a basement or attic*

- *A magical land is being taken over by a great, dark evil*

- *A loyal pet dog comes along on the quest*

- *A wise person knows how to defeat the evil but is too old to go on the quest*

- *A magic item is the only way to defeat the evil*

PRO TIP

A bunch of good ideas can turn what seems like a weak first idea into gold. When you think about it, Batman—a guy who dresses up as a bat to fight thugs—is kinda ridiculous. But he's been in some amazing stories. By giving him a serious backstory and the Joker as an enemy, the creator sets up a great contrast in characters.

The key to success is to come up with lots of ideas—even bad ones can turn out amazing when paired with the right ideas.

These ideas sound familiar, right? That's because they're used over and over again. But what if you came up with **your own spin** on them?

- *A kid discovers that his adoptive parents have superpowers, but he has none and isn't welcome on their adventures...at least not until he proves he doesn't need superpowers to be useful*

- *The promise of a world-saving amulet was a lie told by the evil villain disguised as a helpful wizard—and now the heroes have to find their own solution*

- *The pet dog turns out to be a spy for the evil villain*

- *The magic portal is the front door to the house, and the whole family goes on the adventure...along with the mailman*

A FINAL THOUGHT:

Coming up with ideas is a skill you must practice like any other

Be an active thinker—don't just read a story, think about why it works. Use moments from your life, your imagination, and other people's stories to build comics in directions that no one else has explored.

YOUR TURN

BEING CREATIVE

Do you have a thinking cap?
Maybe a thinking shoe? Lucky underwear?
Well, put them on and get your brain fired up!

1 Keep notes for a <mark>week of all of the interesting ideas you think of.</mark>
See if you can turn any of them into comics. If you can't, try again
the next week.

2a. Use the "magic if" technique (page 62) to make a short comic with a
character in at least three of these scenarios. You can use the list of
characters on page 55 if you're stuck. <mark>Or you could brainstorm.</mark>

- Lost in a forest
- Caught cheating on a test
- Attacked by a vampire
- Making dinner
- Decorating a room
- Picking a Halloween costume
- Waiting in a long, long line
- Raining ice cream

- Thinking about changing their "look"
- Winning the lottery
- Bumping into a famous actor or musician
- Composing a love note
- Accepting an award
- Discovering their lunch can talk
- Making a time capsule
- Getting ready for bed

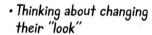

b. Now come up with three of your own "magic if" scenarios — one from normal life, one from the news, and one completely zany idea. Make a short comic with your character in each of those scenes.

c. Repeat a and b with another very different character.

d. Repeat a and b with a real person you know (it could be you).

3 Choose a fictional character and draw a two-page comic that is a journal of her typical day. When does she wake up? What does she eat for breakfast? Who are her friends or family? How does she relax? Questions like these can help you understand your character better.

4 a. Make a list of at least ten examples for three of the following:

- Settings in the city
- Settings in the wilderness
- Types of clothing
- Foods that have double meanings
- Distinguishing marks

- Personality quirks
- Pet peeves
- Time periods that interest you
- Unusual pets
- Unusual jobs

b. Make a comic inspired by one of the examples.

UNUSUAL JOBS

5 Make your own word list about a topic you'd like to draw. Then make two comics based on the ideas you come up with.

6 Make your own doodles for a topic you'd like to draw. Then make two comics based on the ideas you come up with.

7a. Make a list of at least four tropes from any genre (these are characters or situations that are often used). Below is a list of genres to get you thinking. Make a comic based on one of the tropes you come up with.

- Romantic comedy
- Spy
- Superhero
- Martial arts
- Cops and robbers
- Family drama
- Two people swap bodies
- Dance or music contest

- Underdog sports team
- Fantasy with elves or dwarves
- Sci-fi in the near future
- Sci-fi with aliens
- Child detective
- Reality TV drama
- Natural disaster

SUPERHERO

- A SECRET IDENTITY THAT CAN'T BE SHARED, EVEN WITH CLOSE FAMILY

- A RECKLESS SIDEKICK, SO THE HERO CAN TEACH RESPONSIBILITY LESSONS

- THE POLICE ARE USELESS AGAINST SUPER VILLAINS

b. Now come up with a twist on a trope. Make another comic about the twist.

8 Go back to the Your Turn section in Secret Two (pages 30–31). You made a mash-up of genres to inspire new stories. Can you use your new brainstorming techniques to help make your mash-up into a great story?

PRO TIP

How many times have you been enjoying a video game, movie, or comic and thought, "It would be awesome if this happened next!" …aaannnd then it doesn't. Make a note of the idea and then use it to write that story yourself!

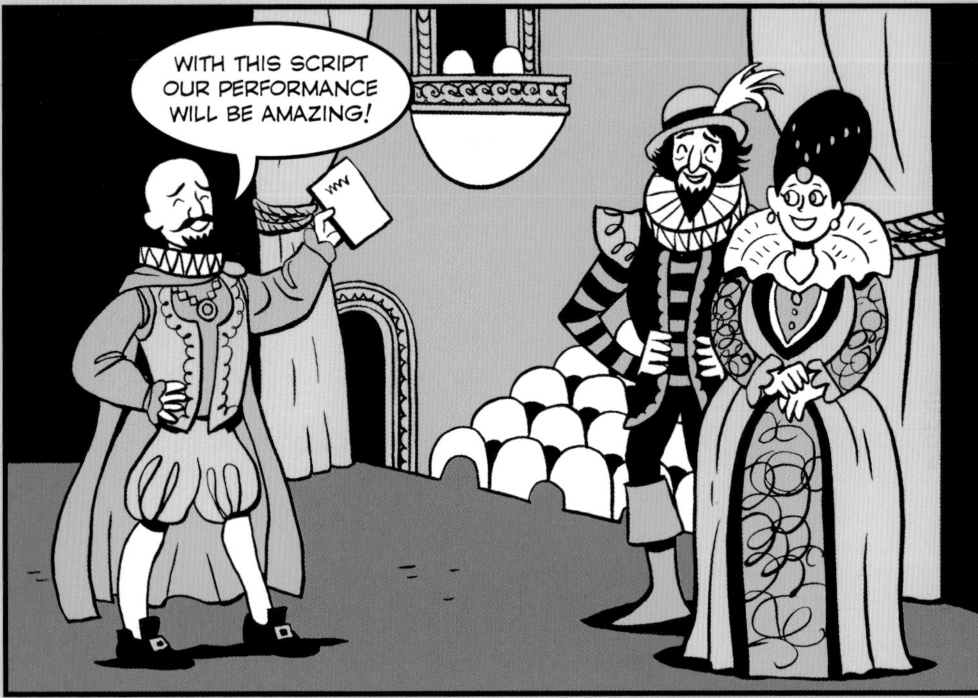
WITH THIS SCRIPT OUR PERFORMANCE WILL BE AMAZING!

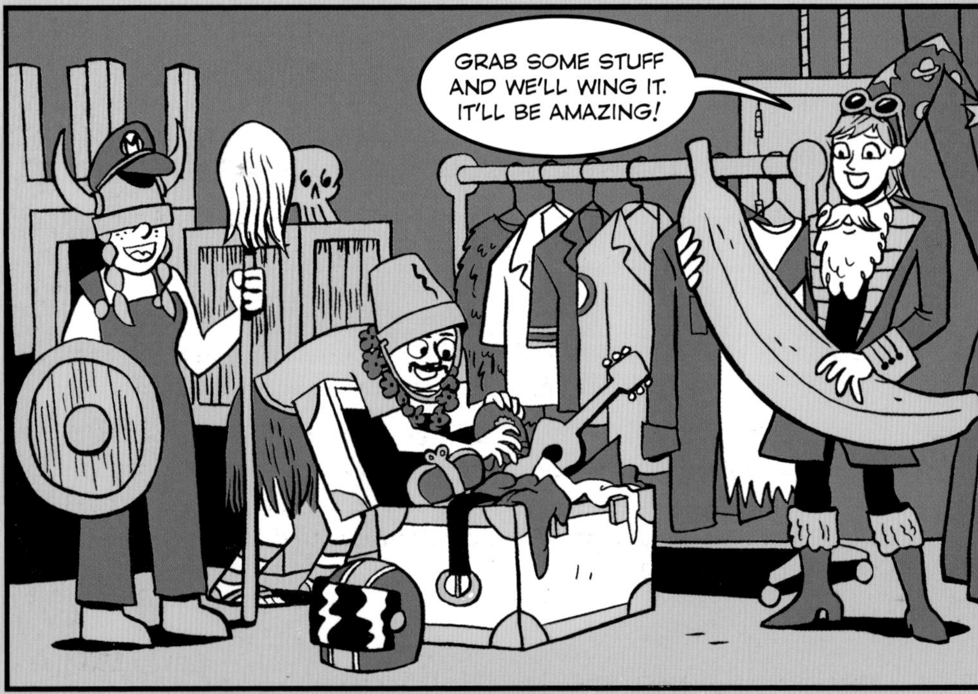
GRAB SOME STUFF AND WE'LL WING IT. IT'LL BE AMAZING!

there are 2 WAYS to tell a STORY

Once your inspiration and ideas have been collected, you're ready to build your story. Will you follow a blueprint? Or just make it up as you go along?

Many comics have a sort of **blueprint** called a **plot**. A plot lets you know where most of the pieces of your story will go before you start drawing it.

But things don't always have to go according to a plan! You can also build a comic by putting down interesting **pieces of story** without knowing how it will end. Each of those pieces is called a **vignette** (pronounced *vin-yet*). This might sound crazy, but many comics are made up of hundreds or even thousands of vignettes.

Plot-based stories show a **big chunk** of time. They begin with a problem and end with it being solved. Here's a really short one.

Vignettes pick a **small moment** to share with the reader.

The main differences: plot vs. vignettes

For a plot-based story, a writer has a beginning and end in mind. The story's main problem is often a big one, like the Earth being invaded by aliens. The main character usually learns a life-changing lesson by the end of the story. Examples of plot-based stories can be found in movies, novels, and graphic novels.

For a vignette, a writer creates characters and a setting and then lets them go about their lives. The characters may face problems, but these are more everyday events, like staying out late on a school night or discovering a new food. Most of these situations don't change the characters' personalities much. Examples of vignettes include sitcoms, soap operas, and comic strips.

114

The plot thickens

Most great plot-based stories have **more than one conflict.** Usually there's one conflict experienced by the main character and another experienced by the world around him. The conflicts often overlap, like they do here for Spider Spy.

Spider Spy has to deal with his ex-girlfriend *and* save the world from Sgt. Skull. There's an **inner** conflict and an **outer** one...and the hero has to face them both. That makes it more interesting to the reader. How? Look at the two examples below.

This just isn't as powerful as...

Spoiler alert!!!

Every good conflict needs a **good resolution**. When the inner problems are solved, the outer ones are, too—but not before we doubt the outcome. Doubt is important because it makes us nervous about whether the hero will succeed. Let's look at some classic plot resolutions.

Star Wars

Conflict: Luke is afraid that he's like his evil dad.

Doubt: Luke's hand is replaced with a mechanical one...just like his dad's!

Resolution: Evil dad saves son, taking down the even-more-evil bad guy himself.

Why it works: Luke sees that being like his dad isn't all bad.

Lord of the Rings

Conflict: Frodo is afraid the evil ring is too much for him to bear.

Doubt: Frodo calls the ring "my precious" just like Gollum did.

Resolution: Sam helps Frodo withstand the ring's power and complete his quest.

Why it works: It shows that real strength comes from our friends.

Spider-Man

Conflict: Peter's not sure how to use his superpowers to benefit himself.

Doubt: His lack of heroism results in his uncle Ben's death.

Resolution: He becomes a superhero to the benefit of others.

Why it works: It shows that being given great power is a challenge we can rise to meet.

Don't rip off your readers

The important thing about a resolution is that it feels satisfying. It doesn't have to be the best possible outcome for the hero—or the world— but it shouldn't make the reader feel like the story was a waste of time.

If Darth Vader had killed Luke and the rebels had been defeated, that would be pretty crummy. After the first two films had pushed the message that evil could be overcome, that ending would say "Nope! Just kidding!" Bummer.

Sure, surprise endings can be great, but think of surprise parties—you wouldn't want one where the "surprise" is a kick in the pants and half a used lollipop. You want a **satisfying surprise**.

So going back to Spider Spy, maybe it could end with a twist like this?

AMY ALSO ASKED ME TO CHOOSE BETWEEN HER AND SAVING THE WORLD.

THIS TIME I CHOSE BOTH. I DISARMED THE MISSILES AN HOUR AGO.

What goes in the middle?

If plot-based stories are like blueprints, then the main characters, conflicts, and resolutions give you the structure of your building. When you're filling in extra pieces (like secondary characters or twists in the story), it should be easy to tell if these new pieces fit or not—like adding more bricks to open spaces in your building's frame.

A typical middle finds your hero trying to solve the conflict and failing. Then the **hero can learn** from these mistakes—and grow as a character—before winning in the end.

The middle parts can also have your hero needing to accomplish a few smaller goals before being able to solve the final problem.

As long as you arrive at the ending you want, and stay true to the story, anything can happen.

Who's the main character?

Some stories are inspired by a character you want to write about. Great! But what if you're not sure who is the lead?

Let's say you wanted to tell a story about an underdog sports team that wins the championship. How do you know which team member is the main character? The one who has the most at stake! Maybe she used to be on last year's winning team but got sent to the minors and traded before the championship? Now she's on the last-place team and trying to prove her worth. Explore your characters as you create them to see who's the best fit.

We all have conflicts in our lives

Personal conflicts can inspire great comics. We have conflicts with villains, like bullies, or with friends when we compete for the same prize. Or with nature, when we are bitten by bugs while camping. Or with ourselves, like when we have to choose between finishing our homework or doing something else.

When we tell plot-based stories about our own lives, the problems we choose are the important ones. They might not be as important to the rest of the world as Sgt. Skull and his missiles, but they are important to us. Can you think of plot-based stories from your life?

These two panels might be the beginnings of some plots you can relate to.

Vignettes: Let's hang out

Some stories aren't about solving problems as much as they're about sharing moments. If vignettes have conflicts, they are usually not nearly as important as the ones in plot-based stories. And the resolution comes much quicker—plus, it may not even solve anything important.

Instead, vignettes are really about **spending time** with your characters as if they were your friends and family. Imagine some vignettes about friends playing a game of cards. Rather than focusing on a bigger conflict, like who will win a game of Crazy Eights, the comic can just record strategies used in the game.

Or something funny that happened during the game.

Or how the characters felt about the way the game ended.

Each vignette is a little story. Put together enough vignettes with the same characters, and they might build up into a plot-based story—they just take a less direct route to get there. In these three examples, the third comic does actually show the end of the card game conflict. But the first two comics don't seem to care about that ending at all.

In the same boat

If characters in vignettes don't grow or change much, how do they stay interesting? First, you give 'em personalities that will **create conflicts** with their fellow characters. Second, you come up with a setting that keeps them all together—even if they don't get along very well! That's why vignette characters are often "stuck in the same boat," such as a family, classroom, sports team, or neighborhood. Even if they travel to new places together, they don't get to split up.

Personality traits

Each main character should have a few traits that give you a variety and contrast of behavior. For instance, the characters on the previous pages could be summed up with:

Ann: *loves math, gullible*   **Al:** *very practical, suspicious*   **Mike:** *always hungry, tricky*

Maybe you can imagine Ann's math skill saves her from gullibly believing one of Mike's tricks to get her food?

Goal!!!

Another great way to define characters is by their goals. Then you know what **each person wants** out of any situation. For instance, you could make up goals like these:

- *Always/never wants attention of the group*
- *Always/never wants to take on responsibility*
- *Always/never makes things into a joke*

122

Then combine them into three people. Let's make them all superheroes.

Cape Ape:
Always wants attention, never responsible

Miss Mystery:
Always makes jokes, never wants attention

Captain Hero:
Always responsible, never makes jokes

Next, use the "magic if" to put them in a situation. For example, what if they all played a game of Crazy Eights?

Your characters can be inspired by a variety of things, like star signs, music genres, favorite animals, or family and friends. Then pick a setting you know something about. If you choose these things well, you'll find your vignettes almost begin to write themselves.

The Robot, the Animal, the Child

The most common trio of characters in comedy is called the Robot, the Animal, and the Child. The characters don't have to actually be robots, animals, or children—it's more about how they behave.

- *The Robot lacks emotion but is logical and smart*
- *The Animal is passionate and acts without thinking*
- *The Child doesn't get what's going on, occasionally in a brilliant way*

In the Powerpuff Girls, Blossom is the robot, Buttercup is the animal, and Bubbles is the child. In what other comedies can you find this trio?

This feels real

Why do we like vignettes? They are a lot like how we experience life. There are some stories in our lives with beginnings and endings, but most of the time we don't feel like we're part of a plot-based story. Sure, there are broken hearts and bad apples, but there are also a lot of chores and relaxing.

Even though vignettes feel real, that doesn't mean they have to be. You *could* do a diary comic, but you could also do one about a robot making rainbows. Even if you make up your whole story, people might think you've based it on real people and events. That's the power of vignettes.

Stand-alone vignettes

Sometimes, vignettes aren't part of a long series with the same characters. Most of the jokes you know are stand-alone vignettes. One might be about a duck buying ChapStick and another about a genie granting wishes. You can use vignettes to share ideas, jokes, or other things besides moments in a character's life.

Stand-alone vignettes use a lot of costumes. When you don't have the same characters in each comic, you need to be clear about who the duck is talking to, or why someone has the power to grant wishes.

A FINAL THOUGHT:
Which is right for you?
Some people like their stories to go from A to B to C. Some prefer to improvise and let characters wander from Z to H to 11. Whether you pick plots or vignettes for your comics is up to you. Which style do you think will suit you best?

YOUR TURN

PLOTS AND VIGNETTES

There may be two basic ways to tell a story, but there are lots of stories to tell. These suggestions might help you on your way.

1a. Write down ten conflicts you've had in the past and how they were resolved. The conflicts can be with a person, yourself, or nature.

b. Write the plot points of one of those conflicts as if you had to make it into a story. Like this:

- Parents told me not to stay up late while they were out.

- I stayed up late to finish a level on my video game. Then another.

- Then I tried to fall asleep, but I was still too amped up from gaming and felt guilty about not going to bed on time.

- Next morning, I was tired. I admitted that I stayed up late.

- My folks appreciated my honesty and forgave me.

2 Write down inner conflicts, resolutions, and why they worked for ten of your favorite stories. Are there any patterns to the types of conflicts or resolutions you enjoy?

3 Children's fairy tales usually only stress outer conflict. Decide how you could focus on inner conflict in three different fairy tales. Does Cinderella worry that even in fancy clothes, she won't be appreciated by the prince? Write down notes for each. You can turn them into comics if you are inspired.

4 Make a list of **ten things you do at least once a week.** For all ten things, list each step in the process as if you were writing instructions for someone who had never done it before. Turn one of them into a comic. See if your friends find it entertaining.

5 Draw a short vignette comic that **shares something unique** you've experienced in the past week.

6 Draw five short vignettes about things that happened to you that **build into a longer story.** You might write about:

- A summer at camp
- Your first job
- Your favorite holiday
- An embarrassing moment
- A dream you had

- Your first week at a new school
- A contest you entered
- Something you built
- Doing chores
- A game you played

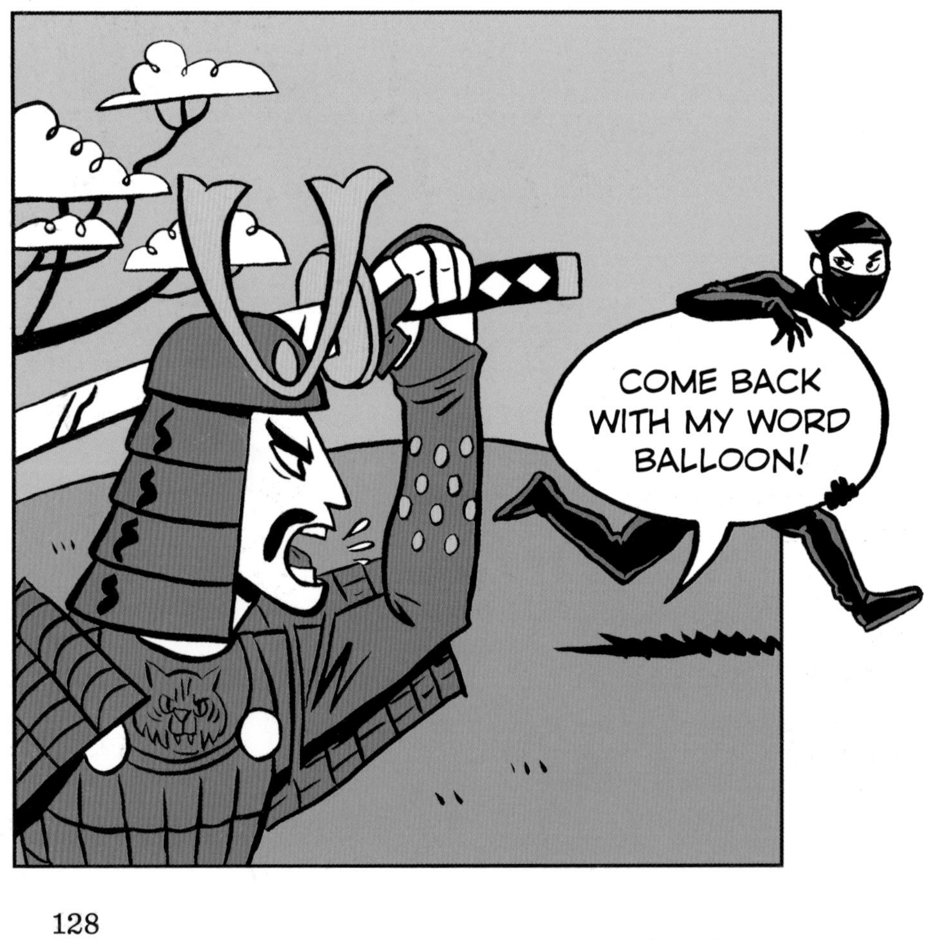
COME BACK WITH MY WORD BALLOON!

GO BEYOND the NORMAL

Comics don't have to tell stories about regular things in regular ways. Let your imagination spark creative ways to tell each story.

If a reader can believe a stick figure is a person, then a stick dragon or stick transforming robot car should look just as real. As long as your chosen style stays consistent, you'll be fine. It's only when you place a realistic picture beside a fake one that things look weird. See?

And since you can draw anything you like, you should consider **drawing more** than just everyday things.

Making an impression

Photographs tell you what a person *looks* like. Cartoony art tells you what person *is* like. It's like **doing an impression** of someone. You exaggerate a character's behavior and features. What details come to mind when you close your eyes and think of these characters?

Metaphors are comparisons of similarity

We use metaphors all the time. You could say the rainfall was a drumroll on the roof. Or that the rain was a dark curtain. Sometimes we use metaphors without even thinking, such as "a blanket of snow." They are especially great for describing something like love or pain, when simple words can't do the job.

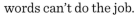

Those are verbal metaphors, but with comics you get to use visual metaphors. What if we told a story about a character who was a ghost? That could mean the character was invisible or scary.

130

In this case, the other characters around the ghost could be normal people, or they could also be visual metaphors. In fact, most of our non-human characters represent people. For instance, a werewolf can be someone who is two-faced: nice when you're around and mean when you're not.

Visual metaphors are like costumes that go to an even deeper level.

You're an animal

The most common comic metaphor for characters is the animal. Why? Because we share more traits with them than we do with floating brains and fruit. It doesn't matter what color your skin is or how old you are, you might be able to see yourself as a bit like a cat, dog, or bear.

We use animal metaphors all the time, insulting people with words like "snake" or complimenting them with "work horse." Like most metaphors, though, the **same word** can represent **different things** depending on how they're used.

An animal can have more than one trait. It's up to you to decide which one works best for a character.

You can use props and settings as metaphors as well.

A magical conductor

A crowded ant-farm office

Why metaphors?

Metaphors allow you to make the point of your story less obvious. A reader might be halfway through a ghost story before she guesses "this is a story about being being ignored by others." A great story comes first, and the message comes second.

You can use active reading to find metaphors in comics. Think about the superhero team X-Men. They were named the X-Men after their leader, Professor Xavier. But what else could the "X" mean? Do any of these make sense to you? Can you think of any more?

- *They are mutants who are no longer men and therefore ex-men.*

- *People sign their name "X" to hide their identity. Cyclops, Rogue, and the rest of the group use code names to hide their identity.*

- *Maps show treasure with an "X." The mutants treasure the home they have found with other mutants.*

And even if readers don't get the same message you wanted them to get, it's okay. Metaphors encourage people to read deeper into stories, which is a good thing. It's also cool that a metaphor makes reading and creating comics into a kind of game. It's a bonus puzzle for readers to solve—or not—as they please.

Allusions

Allusions are references to another story, event, person, or place. They let you **borrow** from a great story to lend **power** to your own.

For instance, if you had a high school as your main setting, your choice of name for the school could hint at what sort of story you're telling.

What if you want to make a story about vampires? You could:

- *Name it after a famous vampire: "Dracula High"*
- *Name it after Dracula's author: "Bram Stoker High"*
- *Name it after Dracula's house: "Carfax High"*

The challenge with allusions is that if someone gets them too quickly, they can seem cheesy. But if some readers don't get them at all, they can seem like a waste. Don't worry about it. Not every reader will get every allusion. We all have different experiences.

Make it visual

Comics can also use visual allusions. You can draw something that looks like another famous image.

When the vampires terrify someone at the school, you could have the person strike the pose from *The Scream*, the famous painting by Edvard Munch.

Or you could draw the school's main heroes, who fight the vampires and werewolves, to resemble other famous heroes. Maybe Little Red Riding Hood or Superman?

The key is to just **hint** at other stories and characters—not to outright copy them.

Keep it moving

It may seem silly to have superheroes chat while they fly through the city or clobber villains. That's because in real life, it's hard to hear someone from a few feet away, never mind them being out of breath and talking from behind a mask. But comics are visual, and they are more fun to draw—and look at—when interesting stuff is going on. Just look at this comparison.

Here's the same scene twice. First, with no setting or action (a bit dull).

Now again, with the characters doing something (more interesting).

You may find that placing your characters in a setting helps you continue the story, too. Maybe this competition for a guy turns into a foot race?

Plus, moving your characters around means that the background in the panel changes—and that you don't have to redraw the same room (and all of the props in that room) over and over. What a relief!

Break the rules!

This book is full of suggestions and rules for telling stories with comics. But breaking the rules is important...and also fun! Of course, you still need to learn the rules so you **know when** to break them to help tell your story.

For instance, most of the time comic panels are plain boxes that hold the drawings. That's good. You want the *inside* of the box to be interesting. It's like a TV. If the frame of your TV changed colors, textures, and shapes, that would make it harder to focus on the show. But *sometimes* those kinds of **changes can be used** to make the story better...

How about panels that double as a city's buildings?

Breaking rules is all about thinking outside the box!

The same thing's true with color, word balloons, sound effects, and everything else in comics grammar. You get to explore all sorts of new ways to bend the rules.

You can have some fun with word balloons...

...or maybe sound effects will be where you play around?

A FINAL THOUGHT:

Comics tell visual stories

Not every story needs to use a metaphor or allusion or to break the rules. But thinking about and exploring your visual options can make an ordinary comic an extraordinary one.

CRAZY IDEAS

OK, everyone. 3, 2, 1...
let's get bɹiɘw!

1a. Draw you and three people you know as metaphors (page 130–131).

b. Do the same with four famous people.

c. Do the same with four fictional characters.

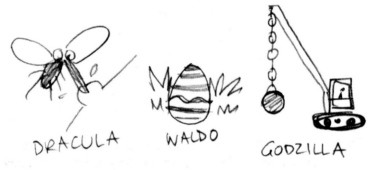

DRACULA

WALDO

GODZILLA

3 MUSKETEERS

FRANKENSTEIN'S MONSTER

TASMANIAN DEVIL

2 Come up with a list of twenty names (they can include characters, groups, or places). Try to think of interesting metaphors for as many of the names as you can.

3 Draw a comic that shows how you feel about school using a verbal metaphor and a visual metaphor.

4 a. Pick ten animals and list two traits that describe each.

b. Draw five of these animals as characters with those traits.

5 a. Come up with a name for a high school set in a romance story, a sci-fi story, a mystery story, and a comedy. Each should contain an allusion.

b. Choose one of those high schools (or use one of the vampire ones from page 133) and come up with the names for the principal, homeroom teacher, and main student. They should all be allusions.

6 Draw four people that resemble famous characters, without making them look exactly alike. See if people pick up on the allusion.

and AWAY YOU GO!

You now know the ten secrets of making comics.
You can get to work on your own very awesome cartoons.
If you get stuck on something, you can always come back
to the book to find some help.

You can even repeat the activities, like exercises that
keep you in great shape. The key to getting good at
anything is to do it a lot. So try to make comics every day,
and sooner, rather than later, you'll be amazing at it.

If you're not sure what to do with your comics, here are
a few suggestions.

- Give them away as cards or presents on birthdays
  or holidays

- Photocopy them into booklets for a zine fair or
  comic convention

- Share them on a website

- Try to publish them in your school newspaper
  or yearbook

- Ask your teacher if you could do a book report
  or essay in comic form

The fun is just beginning.

WHEN I WENT TO COLLEGE FOR ILLUSTRATION, I WANTED TO DO MORE THAN DRAW PICTURES. I WANTED TO DRAW STORIES.

SOME CLASSMATES SHOWED ME THAT COMICS WERE EXACTLY THAT. BUT THERE WAS NO COURSE TO TEACH ME COMICS AT THE TIME.

TODAY, MANY COURSES EXIST, BUT THEY FOCUS MORE ON THE DRAWING THAN THE STORYTELLING.

THAT'S WHY I WANTED TO MAKE MY OWN GUIDE, TO SHARE ALL THE SECRETS I LEARNED FROM MAKING COUNTLESS COMICS.

COMICS MAY BE OVER A HUNDRED YEARS OLD, BUT THEY ARE BECOMING MORE RELEVANT THAN THEY'VE EVER BEEN.

SO WELCOME TO THE PARTY. THERE'S ROOM FOR ALL OF US TO DRAW OUT THE STORY!

INDEX

ACKNOWLEDGEMENTS

The idea that painting excels at showing detail for one moment in time and writing excels at showing time passing comes from University of Toronto professor Nick Mount's adapted theory of Gotthold Ephraim Lessing in *Laocoon*.

The observations that humans identify better with iconic images and the descriptions of how timing works in comic panels are from Scott McCloud's groundbreaking *Understanding Comics*. In fact, he was one of the only people really dissecting comics when I wanted to learn all about them.

The idea of brainstorming using separate categories and including opposites comes from Gene Perret's *Comedy Writing Step by Step: How to Write and Sell Your Sense of Humor*.

And obviously, the "magic if" comes from Constantin Stanislavski.

I also want to thank a friend I met at college who got me back into comics and has always been full of insight: J. Bone. Check out his *Gobukan* webcomic.

And to my wife, Amber, who has understanding, patience, and a case of the hilarious.